Submarine Warfare in World War II: The History of the Fighting Under the Waves in the Atlantic and Pacific Theaters

By Charles River Editors

A picture of British officers on a destroyer that's part of a convoy searching for German submarines

About Charles River Editors

Charles River Editors provides superior editing and original writing services across the digital publishing industry, with the expertise to create digital content for publishers across a vast range of subject matter. In addition to providing original digital content for third party publishers, we also republish civilization's greatest literary works, bringing them to new generations of readers via ebooks.

Sign up here to receive updates about free books as we publish them, and visit Our Kindle Author Page to browse today's free promotions and our most recently published Kindle titles.

Introduction

Submarine Warfare in the Atlantic

A picture of a German sub hitting a merchant ship with torpedoes

"We in the tower were given a chance to view the holocaust. Three vessels lay heavily listing, shooting smoke and fire columns into the air. White lifeboats hung head-down in their davits. Two destroyers raced toward the dying ships. It was a painting of rare and vivid colors." – U-boat commander Herbert A. Werner, describing a submarine attack in August 1941 (Werner, 2002, 53).

Danger prowled under both the cold gray waters of the North Sea and the shimmering blue waves of the tropical Atlantic during World War II as Adolf Hitler's Third Reich attempted to strangle Allied shipping lanes with U-boat attacks. German and British submarines combed the vast oceanic battlefield for prey, while scientists developed new technologies and countermeasures.

Submarine warfare began tentatively during the American Civil War (though the Netherlands and England made small prototypes centuries earlier, and the American sergeant Ezra Lee piloted the one-man "Turtle" vainly against HMS Eagle near New York in 1776). Britisher Robert Whitehead's invention of the torpedo introduced the weapon later used most frequently by submarines. Steady improvements to Whitehead's design led to the military torpedoes deployed against shipping during both World Wars.

World War I witnessed the First Battle of the Atlantic, when the Kaiserreich unleashed its U-boats against England. During the war's 52.5 months, the German submarines sent much of the British merchant marine to the bottom. Indeed, German reliance on U-boats in both World War I and World War II stemmed largely from their nation's geography. The Germans eventually recognized the primacy of the Royal Navy and its capacity to blockade Germany's short coastline in the event of war. While the British could easily interdict surface ships, submarines slipped from their Kiel or Hamburg anchorages unseen, able to prey upon England's merchant shipping.

During World War I, German U-boats operated solo except on one occasion. Initially, the British and nations supplying England with food and materiel scattered vessels singly across the ocean, making them vulnerable to the lone submarines. However, widespread late war re-adoption of the convoy system tipped the odds in the surface ships' favor, as one U-boat skipper described: "The oceans at once became bare and empty; for long periods at a time the U-boats, operating individually, would see nothing at all; and then suddenly up would loom a huge concourse of ships, thirty or fifty or more of them, surrounded by a strong escort of warships of all types." (Blair, 1996, 55).

World War I proved the value of submarines, ensuring their widespread employment in the next conflict. Besides Germany and Britain, Japan and the United States also built extensive submarine fleets before and/or during the war. One critical innovation in World War II's Atlantic U-boat operations consisted of wolf-pack tactics, in which Admiral Karl Dönitz put great faith: "The greater the number of U-boats that could be brought simultaneously into the attack, the more favourable would become the opportunities offered to each individual attacker. [...] it was obvious that, on strategic and general tactical grounds, attacks on convoys must be carried out by a number of U-boats acting in unison." (Dönitz, 1990, 4).

However, even the wolf-pack proved insufficient to defeat the Atlantic convoys and stop Allied commerce – the precise opposite of the Pacific theater, where America's excellent submarine forces annihilated much of Japan's merchant marine and inflicted severe damage on the Imperial Japanese Navy.

Submarine Warfare in the Pacific

A Picture of Makin Island Taken from the USS *Nautilus*

"When we went out on patrol we were on our own. There was no one to give us orders how to make the approach, how to attack, how to follow through. It was us against the enemy. We were corsairs in a world that had almost forgotten the word." – George Grider

Submarines exercised a decisive impact on the outcome of the Pacific Theater in World War II. The U.S. submarine fleet, largely though not exclusively under the overall command of Vice Admiral Charles Lockwood, strangled the supply lines and shipping traffic of the Empire of Japan. Their commerce raiding crippled both Japan's ability to keep its frontline units supplied and to manufacture the weapons, vessels, and vehicles needed to successfully carry on the struggle.

The United States and Japan both produced excellent, high-tech submarines in the context of the World War II era. Japanese I-boats showed excellent seakeeping capabilities and offered the versatility created by their large size, including the ability to serve as motherships for midget submarines or aircraft carriers for scouting aircraft or even specialized bombers. The Type 93 Long Lance and Type 95 torpedoes they carrier packed enough punch to sink capital ships like battleships and carriers at ranges of several miles.

American submarines, though smaller, could dive deeply, move quickly, and provide both firepower and survivability. Though their Type XIV and Type XVIII torpedoes could not match the Japanese Type 93, they still gave a lethal punch, particularly after improvements in late 1943. The *USS Archerfish* demonstrated the deadliness of American submarines to Japanese capital ships also.

The submariners of both fleets showed immense courage, daring, and skill in carrying out their duties. Both groups of men exhibited aggression, patriotism, and fighting spirit in equal measure, regardless of the different cultural lenses through which these traits manifested themselves. Both navies successfully produced professional, highly capable submarine officers.

The Japanese, however, decided to use their submarines mainly to support a grand fleet action at visual ranges, which never occurred. Instead, the submarines carried out sporadic, uncoordinated attacks and the rest of the time remained on sentry duty or found their time squandered with supply runs and undersea evacuations.

The Japanese never corrected these problems – probably due to cultural factors. The rowdy, democratic Americans, suspicious of authority and used to asserting themselves, confronted their commanders boisterously when they felt something was amiss. The torpedo problem nearly caused fistfights between submarine skippers and admirals, yet in the end, the admirals examined and corrected the problem.

Though constituting only 1.6% of the total U.S. Navy's tonnage in the Pacific, the submarine fleet inflicted massive losses on the Imperial Japanese Navy and Japan's crucial merchant marine. Submarines sank 55% of the merchant shipping lost, or approximately 1,300 vessels; overall, the Allies sank 77% of Japan's shipping.

The submarines also sank 214 Japanese warships, including 82 of 1,000 tons or more – 4 carriers, 4 escort carriers, one battleship, 4 heavy cruisers, 9 light cruisers, 38 destroyers, and 23 submarines – or approximately 30% of the entire Imperial Japanese Navy. The sleek, predatory craft made in the shipyards of Virginia, Wisconsin, or Washington state devastated the naval and freighter assets of the Empire of the Rising Sun out of all proportion to their numbers, at a cost of 42 submarines on "Eternal Patrol."

Submarine Warfare in World War II: The History of the Fighting Under the Waves in the Atlantic and Pacific Theaters analyzes the underwater fighting between the Allies and Axis across the oceans. Along with pictures of important people, places, and events, you will learn about submarine warfare like never before.

Submarine Warfare in the Atlantic

The Importance of the Atlantic

The fighting for control of the Atlantic represented an arms race on multiple levels, including both offensive weapons systems and defensive countermeasures. While the Allies honed their convoy technology and improved its use, the Germans added new features to their U-boats, enabling them to move faster, hit harder, and attempt to escape after an attack in a more effective manner. The back-and-forth exchange witnessed the Germans discovering a fresh weakness, exploiting it, and then, after a brief period of notable success, losing ground to new countermeasures. In this race, the Allies eventually outpaced the Axis, leading to the effective defeat of the U-boats and their reduction to a mere annoyance later in the war.

The stakes of this naval struggle remained very high throughout the war. America's control of the sea lanes provided Britain with food and weaponry, while the Lend-Lease program supplied the Soviets with materiel without which their defeat would have been nearly assured. Alongside tens of thousands of trucks, locomotives, tanks, cars, motorcycles, artillery pieces, 15 million pairs of boots, 14 billion pounds of food (much of it high-calorie processed meat), and countless rounds of ammunition, the Americans also supplied the USSR with a wide range of raw materials, brought in by sea.

Without U.S. control of the sea lanes, the Soviets would have foundered, as the American supply of one vital metal – aluminum – to their quasi-hostile allies demonstrates: "The Soviet Union, however, was desperately short of aluminum. When Harry Hopkins paid his first visit to Josef Stalin in July 1941 to ask the Soviet dictator what the country needed to keep fighting in light of the German invasion, the number one priority he was given was immediate aluminum shipments so that the Soviet Union could build more aircraft. From then until the end of the war, the United States poured aluminum into the Soviet Union. By 1943 it was providing the Soviets more of the metal then was actually allocated to the entire United States Navy." (O'Brien, 2015, 64).

In abandoning the creation of aircraft carriers, the Nazis unwittingly gave up any chance of truly controlling the Atlantic. The U-boats struck like ambush predators, and certain classes of land-based aircraft joined the fray also, but the German lack of aircraft carriers crippled their ability to carry out modern fleet actions and achieve decisive victory at sea.

The Allied commanders already knew from shipping experiences in World War I that large convoys of ships offered a poor target for U-boats. Escorts protected such aggregations of vessels more effectively, concentrating their defensive force and providing mutual support. Therefore, in World War II, convoys provided the rule, not the exception, from the beginning. Though the Germans gained some signal triumphs nevertheless, and nearly halted shipping at a few points, the convoy system married to technological and tactical advances ultimately prevailed.

Even such an apparently simple factor as improving cargo ship engines offered the Allies major dividends. The American and British planners grasped very early that even an extra 1 to 2 knots in speed made a tremendous difference in vessel survivability. Accordingly, the Americans built their Liberty Ships to travel at a then-rapid 11 knots. Over 38 million tons of Liberty Ships launched from American shipyards, amounting to 2,710 ships and overwhelming the U-boats' best efforts by speed and numbers.

As part of the overall strategic plan, Allied command utilized rational statistical analysis, providing invaluable insights into the mathematics behind one of the many factors blending into Allied success in the Atlantic: "The Americans ended up calculating the safety difference of convoys in 1943. [...] One American calculation was that increasing the speed of a convoy from 7 knots to 9 knots gave the ships involved an extra one-third as much protection from German submarine attack.. [...] between October 1942 and May 1943, the faster convoys (those averaging around 9 knots) suffered a 50 percent smaller casualty rate than slower convoys (those averaging around 7 knots), even when they were attacked at approximately the same rate." (O'Brien, 2015, 255-256).

The Germans also utilized surface ships, known as commerce raiders, to strike at the convoys with both cannons and torpedo fire. While it might seem incredible that surface vessels operated openly near the mighty Royal Navy and its constant air patrols, the Nazis managed this trick for some time through clever use of camouflage.

The Germans quickly added and removed false, light wooden structures such as merchant ship funnels or cargo storage bins to rapidly change the appearance of their surface raiders. The British aircraft crews and sailors displayed an almost touching naiveté in the manner in which they accepted some of the Germans' visual hoaxes at face value: "The crews were also trained to wear civilian clothes on deck, and usually there were special 'characters' designed to make the vessel appear more harmless to a casual observer, such as a 'woman' pushing a baby carriage on deck. German disguises fooled British patrols again and again. On May 18, 1941, the *Atlantis* – disguised as a Dutch freighter – passed within 8,000 yards of the British battleship HMS *Nelson* without arousing suspicion." (Forczyk, 2010, 42).

The Germans also set afloat several huge battleships, including the *Bismarck* and the *Graf Spee*. These colossal ships, intended to devastate whole convoys unsupported or with only a handful of other raiders accompanying them, inflicted some damage but ultimately fell victim to their own overwhelming presence. Viewing them as an outsized threat, the British poured all available resources into hunting these battleships down, and their size rendered the ships slow and difficult to hide, sealing their fate once the British successfully pinpointed them with scouting aircraft.

The *Bismarck* famously encountered the British battleships HMS *Hood* and *Prince of Wales* shortly after dawn on May 24th, 1941, but at first the Germans believed the contact to be a much smaller ship. However, the aggressive *Hood* quickly disabused them of the notion: "The fore guns of the Hood woke with a tremendous thunder, the wind swept a huge cloud of black cordite smoke over the bridge and four shells, each weighing more than 800 kilograms, began the 23,000 metre-long journey towards the intended target. All German doubts disappeared as the Hood's guns fired, almost immediately followed by the main guns of the Prince of Wales. The huge muzzle flashes and the long firing range were signs clear enough." (Zettering, 2012, 156).

The *Bismarck*

HMS *Hood*

Following a brief, lethal duel, a probable magazine explosion blew the *Hood* apart, causing it to sink with tremendous loss of life. The *Bismarck's* crew, however, did not long survive to savor their triumph; brought to battle by four British vessels just three days later on May 27th, 1941, the battleship sustained 400 direct hits by shells out of 2,800 fired at it by the English. Seeing his ship set ablaze and unable to escape, the captain ordered the *Bismarck* scuttled, but the British rescued only 111 men before retreating, frightened off by a false report of U-boats approaching. Some 2,200 luckless German sailors drowned or died of exposure in the cold North Sea waters, proving the diminished value of battleships. The *Graf Spee* suffered a similar fate during the Battle of the River Plate in South America.

Despite these high profile battles, Nazi Germany's chief weapon prowled not above the waves but beneath them. The U-boats, used to devastating effect in World War I, returned in an updated form for World War II. In time, over 200 of these craft scoured the Atlantic for targets, striking without warning before slipping away to elude depth charges and other forms of retaliation.

From almost the moment when Britain declared war on Germany following Hitler's 1939 invasion of Poland through 1943, U-boats plied the Atlantic waves, attempting to disrupt Britain's American lifeline. American and Canadian vessels escorted the convoys partway across the ocean before handing over guard duty to British ships. At first, America's lack of war status with the Axis powers ensured this arrangement. Later, the grim but diplomatic U.S. Admiral Ernest J. King continued the practice both to make use of valuable British assets and to respect the patriotic feelings of the English.

King

American support of Great Britain, amounting to a de facto declaration of war against Nazi Germany and the Axis even before Pearl Harbor, enabled the English to remain in the war. Without the weapons, supplies, and material sent across the Atlantic to England, Hitler might perhaps have compelled Winston Churchill's government to accept peace and leave the continent to its Nazi masters. Winston Churchill summed this situation up when he declared "the only thing that really frightened me during the war was the U-boat peril." (Williamson, 2007, 4).

Thus, Nazi Germany's chief answer to the endless convoys streaming across the Atlantic to support its British foes lay in its submarine fleet of U-boats. The Germans, curiously, never developed a fleet of aircraft carriers. The Kriegsmarine began construction of two, the *Graf Zeppelin* and the *Peter Strasser*, but completed neither. Two others never achieved any reality beyond blueprints, while the conversion of a cruiser into the carrier *Weser* began but failed to reach completion.

Other than occasional instances when circumstances allowed them to produce unusual devastation among the convoys, the U-boats of the Kriegsmarine never mustered sufficient force to fully stop the Atlantic convoys. The advent of the Liberty Ships made this event even less likely, given their numbers and relatively high speed. However, Germany's submarines exacted a toll of shipping, materiel, and lives that the Allies found increasingly unacceptable as the tally mounted.

Submarines and Tactics on Both Sides

The submarine warfare occurring in World War II bore little resemblance to the deployment of nuclear submarines in the later 20th and into the 21st centuries. Submarines of all nations operated with diesel engines, not nuclear power plants, thus requiring air to run. For most long-distance cruising, World War II submarines operated at the surface. Attempting to run the diesel engine underwater sucked air out of the living quarters, potentially asphyxiating the crew if run too long.

For underwater operations, submarines carried stacks of large battery cells. These held a limited charge, however; a captain could choose to move quickly but exhaust the batteries in a brief time, or creep along or remain motionless and have power for 16-20 hours of operation. Submarine tactics usually involved moving on the surface until targets appeared, closing at periscope depth, launching torpedoes, and then either escaping underwater or, more often, drifting quietly and hoping to avoid the ferocious counterattack of depth charges until the surface ships gave up and moved away.

A submarine could remain underwater for long periods, but not for an unlimited time. Heat, carbon dioxide, humidity, and fumes from batteries built up steadily until the conditions grew unbearable, then uninhabitable. One American submarine crew in the Pacific set a record by remaining underwater for 63 hours and nearly died from heat exhaustion. Other crews whose submarines vanished likely died a lingering death when they waited too long and could not surface due to exhausted batteries or battle damage.

Submarines operated mostly against surface ships rather than other submarines by their very nature. Surface ships, in turn, possessed an arsenal of weapons suitable for hunting submarines, or at least attempting to sink them in reprisal after an attack.

Anti-submarine warfare remained extremely primitive and largely ineffective during World War I. Lacking sonar technology, only visual sightings of a periscope or a surfaced submarine gave warning of the vessel's proximity. While depth charges developed later in the war, dropping these blind produced few successes.

Ships relied on the hazardous method of attempting to ram if they spotted the submarine at the surface before it fired. While more effective than might be supposed – approximately half of U-boat crews abandoned a given attack after a ramming attempt by their victim – German U-boats nevertheless sank 11 million tons of shipping during the war at very light cost to themselves. The British found themselves driven to measures which might appear risible except for the helplessness and terror motivating them, as British midshipman Stanley M. Woodward reported, "The boom was patrolled at night by two picket boats armed with three-pounder guns and Maxims [machine guns]. The Senior Officer in H.M.S. Exmouth didn't think that this was enough, and ordered each boat to embark two large blacksmiths, armed with flogging hammers, to stand, one on each side of the coxswain. On a periscope being sighted the boat was to steal quietly up alongside it, and the nearest blacksmith was to give it a dint with his hammer!" (McKee, 1993, 48)

World War II witnessed numerous improvements to both hunters and hunted, though the scales tipped ever more heavily against the submarines as the war continued. One of the most important anti-submarine inventions consisted of "ASDIC," or "Anti-Submarine Division" plus "[superson]ic[s]," an early code name for sonar. This sonar device first saw testing in the early 1920s and was in constant use during World War II.

An ASDIC display during World War II

One of ASDIC's peculiarities consisted of a fairly large blind spot directly under the ship carrying the sensor. Accordingly, a destroyer with depth charges could zero in on an underwater submarine until it got close; then the submarine vanished from the sensors. A lethal game of cat and mouse then developed as the submarine attempted to remain quiet and the destroyer crew tried to guess its location and depth, and drop depth-charges accordingly.

Sometimes, lurking submarines endured hours of deafening, terrifying bombardment with depth charges. U-boat commander Herbert A. Werner described the nightmarish conditions aboard a submarine under hours of depth-charge attack: "Distinct splashes on the surface heralded the next spread. A series of 24 charges detonated in quick succession. [...] A new spread deafened us and took our breath away. [...] The steel knocked and shrieked and valves were thrown into open position. [...] The new group launched its first attack, then another, and another. [...] Our nerves trembled. Our bodies were stiff from stress, cold, and fear. [...] The devil seemed to be knocking on our steel hull." (Werner, 2002, 124-125).

In some cases, the submarine survived. In others, depth charge damage forced it to surface, where the crew usually surrendered – or blasts might blow the vessel physically to the ocean surface. In other cases, the submarine suffered fatal damage. The hull might rupture, drowning the crew, or might implode, causing the submarine to sink below its crush depth and crumple in on itself, killing the men aboard with a mix of drowning and crushing water pressure.

Werner also described the incredible relief of surfacing after surviving a prolonged depth charge attack: "U-230 broke through to air and life. [...] Around us spread the infinite beauty of night, sky, and ocean. Stars glittered brilliantly and the sea breathed gently. The moment of rebirth was overwhelming. A minute ago, we could not believe that we were alive; now we could not believe that death had kept his finger on us for 35 gruesome hours." (Werner, 2002, 126).

Later improvements to anti-submarine measures included the Hedgehog anti-submarine mortar. Mounted on the vessel's foredeck, the Hedgehog launched bombs against submarines up to 250 yards ahead of the ship, enabling the vessel to open fire before the submarine entered the ASDIC blind spot. Statistics suggest the Hedgehog proved 10 times more likely to achieve a kill compared to standard depth charges. The Americans later developed the rocket-propelled Mousetrap anti-submarine weapon.

The later German development of an extensive range of midget submarines represented, to some degree, a response to ASDIC. The era's sonar simply could not pick up objects smaller than 40 or 50 feet long, meaning midget submarines enjoyed "invisibility" from ASDIC, despite their many countervailing drawbacks.

`German U-boat design mirrored that of Panzer engineering, with relatively small production runs of numerous variants dominating the scene. Where Allied production focused on building many instances of a few adequate designs, the Third Reich's technicians constantly created experimental vehicles and variations on existing blueprints. While fascinating for military historians, this practice impeded efforts to mass-produce large numbers of even the best designs.

The workhorse of the Kriegsmarine, the Type VII U-boat, represented a medium craft largely obsolete by 1943. In addition to four main variants – the VIIA, VIIB, VIIC, and VIID – the Germans also built the Type VII in minelayer and seven different "flak boat" versions. The Type VII's main advantages included excellent speed and the ability to dive well below the published service depth, offset by a tiny, cramped interior. The Type VII also crash-dived very rapidly, which allowed a quick escape from unexpected attacks but was sometimes so quick that personnel on deck drowned during the crash-dive.

A Type VII U-boat

The Type IX represented the second most common U-boat built – a larger, slower-diving submarine whose advantages included superb seakeeping even in the most violent weather, plenty of elbow room inside, and longer range between refueling halts than the Type VII managed. Once again the Germans produced a number of variants, some of which they manufactured only one example of: the IXA, IXB, IXC, IXC/40, IXD1, IXD2, and IXD2/42, plus a cargo variant.

The specialized Type XIV "Milchkuh," or "milch [ie milk] cow" provided resupply to the other boat types. It carried 400 tons of fuel, plus food, four replacement torpedoes, and a bakery (Williamson, 2005, 52). The Type X, another specialist, laid mines (generally ineffective compared to every other anti-ship weapon).

In the late stages of the war, the Germans introduced the Type XXI, an advanced diesel U-boat designed to counter the new anti-submarine warfare measures of the Allies. This large submarine boasted 6 bow torpedo tubes in place of the usual four and a roomy interior. Its most important feature consisted of a snorkel, however. This device enabled the U-boat to run its diesel engine while submerged, sucking air in through the projecting snorkel. Doing so eliminated most of the U-boat's surface radar profile, enabling rapid movement on diesel power while exposing the vessel far less to aircraft and destroyer detection.

A Type XXI submarine

The Type XXIII presented the characteristics of a smaller Type XXI, with faster crash dives and the ability to operate in shallower coastal waters. In effect, the Type XXIII stood to the XXI as the Type VII did the Type IX.

Meanwhile, the British submarine fleet consisted mostly of three classes, used throughout the war period: the S-class, the T-class, and the U-class. The S-class represented the most numerous submarine in wartime Royal Navy service. In a design tradeoff, the British opted for an expanded prow, which enabled mounting of 6 torpedo tubes but prevented the S-class from diving as deeply as German U-boats due to its relative structural weakness against water pressure (McCartney, 2008, 5).

The T-class submarine represented an excellent design with high reliability combined with an extremely powerful forward array of 10 bow-mounted torpedo tubes. The T-class mounted radar as standard, giving them sensor superiority for their time. T-class submarines eventually sank a confirmed 6 Axis submarines, a notable success considering the rarity of sub-versus-sub battles.

The British also made small U-class submarines. These craft proved successful despite being rather slow – in part due to the 6 torpedo tubes in the bow position. British emphasis on firepower in their submarines at the expense of other characteristics continued in this idiosyncratic design. Due to the small size of the U-class and the large weight of six loaded torpedoes, firing a full spread generally resulted in the U-class vessel popping to the ocean surface like a cork, at least until design changes rectified this problem.

As that quirk suggests, British submarines also took an offensive role during the early part of the war and into the subsequent operational periods. Due to the lower numbers of Axis merchant ships, surface ships, and blockade runners thanks to the Third Reich's control of the European continent's resources, these operations remained less extensive than the U-boat actions.

Both sides also made use of midget submarines. The Germans, true to their design pattern, made close to a dozen different midgets, while the British focused on a single type, the X-class. Though often overlooked, the midgets also appeared around the peripheries of many important operations, such as the sinking of the *Tirpitz* and the D-Day landings.

An X-class midget submarine, photography by Geni

While Japanese midget submarines and suicide torpedoes in the Pacific theater retain the most historical fame, the Allies and Axis both deployed midget submarines in the Atlantic theater. Typical of the Germans, the Kriegsmarine developed a plethora of experimental vessels and subtypes, many of them produced hastily and with little testing as the fortunes of war shifted against the Third Reich.

One of the most ghastly contrivances from the standpoint of the men selected to pilot it consisted of the Neger, or "Negro," a manned torpedo or minimalist midget sub commissioned in 1943 and first deployed at Anzio in March 1944. The Neger's designation derived from a pun on the name of the designer, Richard Mohr, whose last name meant "Moor," a term originally referring to Mauritanians but later applied to all dark-skinned people.

A Neger

The Neger consisted of a metal tube 25 feet long and 21 inches in diameter, containing mostly an engine and fuel. The pilot squeezed into a tiny kayak-like cockpit near the front end, covered by a cramped Plexiglas dome; surviving photos indicate the pilot's head nearly touched the top of this covering. Brackets under the Neger held a G7e torpedo with a 616-lb warhead.

The midget's concept involved cruising at the surface at less than 5 miles per hour until within range of an enemy ship, then lining up the Neger and its underslung torpedo. Pulling a lever then simultaneously released the brackets and started the torpedo motor, sending the ordnance towards the target while the Neger turned around to make its escape.

In practice, the Neger usually presented more of a threat to the courageous operator than to the enemy. The necessity to operate at the surface and the extremely slow speed meant the craft worked best on a calm sea in daylight – precisely the conditions when Allied crews could most easily spot the slow-moving craft and destroy them with deck guns or even small arms fire. Furthermore, even moving at just under 5 mph, considerable wash passed over the Plexiglas dome, partially blinding the operator.

Additionally, the lever sometimes failed to detach the brackets on the underslung torpedo. In these cases, when the G7e's motor started, it carried the Neger and its luckless occupant along on a one-way trip to the target ship's hull, turning the midget into an unintended suicide torpedo. Since a crew bolted the Plexiglas dome in place at launch, escaping the craft before detonation could prove impossible. Even if the pilot successfully broke out through the dome, this left him alone in the water amid hostile vessels.

The first deployment of Negers at Anzio witnessed 37 manned torpedoes launched off fiber mats laid on the beach. 14 immediately sank into the bottom mud, the Germans later destroying them after attempts to refloat the craft failed. Out of the remaining 23, four sank due to mechanical faults, the Allied sailors destroyed four with deck guns, and two fell into Allied hands, with their pilots taken prisoner. Nevertheless, the Negers actually sank a few Allied ships; the remaining 13 managed to sink a light cargo ship and two patrol motorboats.

The men captured included Walter Schulz and Gunther Kuschke. The Americans initially identified the Negers as torpedoes, but they subsequently realized their manned character immediately once lookouts and gun crews noted the telltale Plexiglas domes. USN Captain J.W. Barr described the destruction of Gunther Kuschke's Neger and the capture of the German that ensued: "The 40mm and 20mm [cannons] had registered several hits on this run and the torpedo dived abruptly. We turned hard left and began a sound search, but soon saw an object bob up dead ahead. We assumed it to be the torpedo and opened fire again with the 40mm. As we closed, the object began waving its arms and we knew it was the operator." (Paterson, 2006, 23).

Many late-war manned torpedo and midget submarine pilots belonged to the Waffen SS, and amazingly, the projects remained unknown to the Kriegsmarine command. The Waffen SS sent men under sentence of death to serve in the "K-Verband," or torpedo and midget units, with the understanding that such service provided a full pardon and a "clean slate" if they survived. The men who attacked the ships at Anzio, however, were simply brave sailor volunteers who piloted the craft for ordinary reasons of patriotism and professionalism.

The largest success of the Neger design, albeit one which had a trivial effect on the war overall, occurred in July 1944 when a mixed force of German surface E-boats and 26 Negers attacked several convoys shuttling extra troops to the beachhead in Normandy. On the night of July 5th to 6th, this swarm of manned torpedoes sank two minesweepers, HMS *Magic* and *Cato*. They also destroyed the *Captain*-class frigate HMS *Trollope*, as the ship's Chief Engineer related, though he remained unaware that the lethal torpedo came from a Neger piloted by seaman Walther Gerhold rather than an E-boat: "At around 1 a.m. we started firing star shells at a flotilla of E-boats coming out of Le Havre. We were in an area where we were able to travel no faster than 4 knots because of the danger from oyster mines. From a distance of 3 miles the E-boats fired at us and one of their torpedoes hit us amidships. I was hurled from the flying bridge into the water and in the faint moonlight saw the ship breaking in half." (Collingwood, 1999, 113).

The following night, 21 Negers attacked again, sinking HMS *Pylades*, a minesweeper, and inflicting enough damage on the ORP *Dragon,* a cruiser flying the flag of Poland, to force the ship's scuttling. However, none of the Neger pilots reached Le Havre alive after this foray, since bright moonlight allowed Allied ships and aircraft to hunt the craft down and sink them all. Continued attacks on the Normandy shipping, including one deploying 56 Negers and Marders (an improved Neger design capable of diving for short periods during the approach run), sank six more ships, including two destroyers, through July and early August 1944.

In addition to the Neger, Nazi Germany developed a profusion of other manned torpedo and midget submarine types. Many designs proved duds, but a few saw action and occasional successes. Due to constant experimentation, however, the Kriegsmarine spread its resources too thin. Several excellent midget sub designs received only modest production runs because of the quantity of money, man-hours, and material diverted into the ever-branching maze of side projects.

The Marder represented a sort of "Neger Mark II," featuring much the same design with a small diving tank added to enable ducking briefly beneath the waves up to a depth of 75 feet. The Hai carried the Marder design farther, adding an extended central hull for a larger engine capable of running faster and producing an increased operational range.

A Marder submarine, photographed by Billy Hill at the Bundeswehr Military History Museum Dresden

Other designs proliferated. For example, the Hecht represented a midget submarine with such poor maneuverability that it never saw action, instead serving as a training vessel only, while the Molch, again using a modified torpedo, dived to 120 feet with a 200 foot crush depth, but also lacked agility and suffered heavy losses in action while sinking no ships. The Manta, a two-hull catamaran mini-sub, mounted wheels for launching and recovery, and the Schwertwal (two versions) featured extreme streamlining making underwater speeds of 37 mph possible. The Delphin (two variants) used teardrop streamlining to achieve slightly higher speeds, and several other version with only Type numbers represented attempts to squeeze the design of full-sized U-boats down to midget dimensions. Two further designs saw relatively frequent actual production and use – the Biber (Beaver) and the Seehund ("Seal," literally "Sea Hound"). Of these two, the Seehund proved the superior craft but entered the war too late to realize its full potential.

Kleinſt- Uboot
"Seehund"

Typ XXVIIB

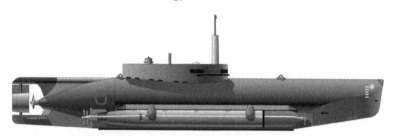

An illustration of the Seehund, by Uwe Ernst

The Biber, a one-man craft resembling a stumpy, almost cartoonish rendition of a full-sized submarine, measured 29 feet long and included a miniature conning tower rather than a Plexiglas dome. The Biber carried two G7e torpedoes as a standard payload, bracketed into scalloped indentations in the lower hull flanks. With the huge torpedoes in place, the Biber looked something like half a hotdog bun between two fat steel hotdogs.

The Germans based many Bibers at the Fecamp basin, though these craft accomplished little beyond suffering approximately 65% casualties from bad weather and Allied air attacks. On December 27th, 1944, an incident at Hellevoitsluis on the Voorneschen Canal demonstrated that the slapdash design of these midgets, combined with the scanty training of their crews, presented another type of danger. Several tugboats towed 14 Bibers into position for launching on a raid against English shipping. One of the Biber pilots – described pithily in the German report as "some idiot" – accidentally fired a torpedo, which ricocheted around the basin, bouncing off seawalls and the lock before running up on the bank and exploding. The blast sent a three-foot high wave across the basin, smashing all the Bibers against the seawall. All of the hatches stood open in readiness for the pilots, allowing the water to flood into the midgets and sink most of them.

The impact of the Bibers striking into each other launched a second torpedo from an unoccupied submarine. This torpedo streaked across the basin to strike one of the tugs, sending it to the bottom and killing five of the crew, plus one Biber pilot. 11 of the 14 Bibers sank, though the last three launched against Allied shipping. Two vanished utterly, while the British recovered the third several days later, drifting with its pilot dead from carbon monoxide poisoning – possibly due to undetected equipment damage inflicted during the accident at Hellevoitsluis.

A Biber, by lokilech

The Kriegsmarine also attempted to use Bibers in a riverine role. A January 1945 effort witnessed a detachment of the midgets attempt the destruction of a critical bridge at Nijmegen, spanning the Waal River, leading to another resounding failure: "Twenty Bibers firing torpedoes equipped with hooks were to clear away any remaining obstructions, followed by four Bibers towing tree trunks from which three-ton mines were suspended. According to Allied after-action and interrogation reports, one Biber was destroyed by artillery fire and seven others ran aground. The road bridge was undamaged." (Prenatt, 2014, 26).

The 39-foot-long Seehund, featuring a two-man crew, took some of its inspiration from captured X-class British midget submarines. A true midget, the Seehund incorporated many characteristics of a full-sized submarine scaled down to a compact hull and a crew of just two individuals. While most of the other German designs included only an electric motor or, in some cases, a dangerously explosive but relatively quiet gasoline engine, the Seehund contained both a diesel engine for surface operations and an electric motor for underwater movement, precisely like a regular U-boat.

The Seehund only entered production in 1944 despite prioritization by Albert Speer. Though the Kriegsmarine planned the construction of 1,000 vessels, only 285 rolled off production lines prior to Germany's surrender.

The first action of the Seehund against British ships proved ignominious. On January 2nd

1945 the destroyer HMS *Cowdray* spotted U-5318, crewed by Werner Hertlein and Rolf Heinze, sitting on the ocean surface and attacked with its deck guns. Though the Seehund attempted to flee, the destroyer's shells smashed its hull open and it sank. Hertlein and Heinze survived uninjured, leaping into the water from the miniature conning tower and soon rescued by the British.

Worse followed as violent weather devastated the initial groups of Seehunds, resulting in the loss of 16 of the 18 craft launched against the British in early 1945. Despite Hitler's exaggerated hopes of sinking 100,000 tons of shipping bringing Allied supplies to Antwerp, the first group of Seehunds sank just one ship, a 324-ton trawler. After that, the K-Verband tried to limit Seehund use to fair weather with low seas.

Over a dozen more Seehund operations followed, but success proved extremely limited and some forays resulted in high losses. U-5330, crewed by Klaus Sparbrodt and Gunter Jahnke, managed one of the midget submarine class' most spectacular successes on January 24th, 1945, near the English coast. After lying on the bottom to avoid the notice of patrolling gunboats, the submarine and its two-man crew surfaced on a fine morning, as Sparbrodt later described: "The sea was mirror-like – sea state 0. […] A slight haze hung over the water and we patrolled up and down at low speed. A little after 10.00hrs […] I saw what looked like a vessel lying stopped […] At 10.20hrs we dived and began our attack. […] I ordered "Port torpedo – fire!" and Jahnke pulled the lever. We heard from the boat's hull a scream and roar as the Eel sped on its way. […] I saw a column of water and smoke from the explosion rising midway between the bridge and funnel. […] We saw the last of the ship as her bow lifted high and she quickly slid stern first into the sea." (Paterson, 2006, 192).

The men sank *La Combattante,* a Free French destroyer, killing 62 of the crew. Though depth charges interrupted their celebratory repast of chicken, rice, and strawberries, the two young Kriegsmarine men successful eluded their opponents and returned safely to their base.

However, such victories eluded most midget sub crews in the war's closing days. Though a handful of other vessels suffered damage or destruction from Seehund or Biber torpedoes, the sinkings proved far too infrequent to even slightly hamper the massive inflow of soldiers, materiel, and supplies into Western Europe during 1944 and 1945.

Despite the lack of success, the Kriegsmarine continued putting resources into the midget submarine program due to the speed of production compared to regular U-boats and the two-man crews needed to operate the vessels, which theoretically increased the number of submarines available even with a declining recruitment pool.

Morale remained high in the K-Verband practically until the end of the war, however. Most of the men, extremely young, came from a highly militarized educational background, simply accepting doing their duty without even thinking to question it. Many enjoyed using the small submarines, despite the cramped, uncomfortable conditions on board, in almost the same way that hobbyists enjoy motorboats or off-road vehicles. Moreover, the Kriegsmarine exempted these men from practically all non-submarine tasks, provided them with superior quality food, housed them as comfortably as the disaster overtaking the Third Reich permitted, and gave them frequent leave periods.

Seehunds operated in the Danube, Rhine, and Oder Rivers, frequently targeting bridges, in the last few months of the war. The craft managed to destroy a few bridges but could not halt the Soviet juggernaut rolling in from the east or the Anglo-American tide sweeping in from the west. Records of these operations remain fragmentary due to the chaos in the dissolving Third Reich military at the time.

The Scandinavia-based K-Verband units surrendered last, in much the same way as the full-sized U-boat units. Due to their ability to avoid Asdic (sonar) thanks to their small size, some Allied commanders expressed relief that the Germans failed to develop the Seehunds sooner. The French took four Seehunds as part of their war reparations and operated them for some time after the war, until the advent of the nuclear submarine eliminated all less efficient designs from the sea.

For their part, the British midget submarines saw less action than their Third Reich counterparts but still served a useful purpose in the war. Due to their small numbers combined with the daring of the missions they undertook, the men who served aboard them received more decorations proportionally than any other branch of the service.

The British used midget submarines in the Atlantic, Mediterranean, and Adriatic during World War II, even sending a few to the Pacific in support of Australia. These X-class submarines, often referred to as X-craft, measured 51 feet in length, considerably larger than many German midget designs. Each carried a crew of four and a standard armament of two 4,400 Amatol high explosive charges.

The carried charges indicate the very different midget submarine doctrine adopted by the British relative to the Germans. The Germans envisioned their midget subs as torpedo-armed hunter-killers, preying on targets of opportunity. The British meant their X-craft to stealthily approach specific, anchored warship targets, place the charges directly beneath the hull, and then retreat before the charges detonated, hopefully rupturing the ship along the keel and sinking it.

Unlike the patched-together German midgets prior to the Seehund, the X-class midget proved a solid, workmanlike vessel, as Commander Richard Compton-Hull described: "The whole thing, out of the water, resembled an old-fashioned railway boiler. In fact, being appointed to command a midget was rather like being given a toy train set for Christmas. It was a perfect submarine in miniature. [...] The 42-horsepower diesel engine that drove the craft on the surface and recharged the battery was the same as that fitted to a London omnibus – it proved just as trustworthy rumbling throatily up the Norwegian fjords as on the streets of the metropolis. Simplicity and ruggedness were the key words." (Howard, 2006, 31-33).

The X-class midgets, mostly built by Vickers-Armstrong Ltd., also featured a different deployment method. While the Germans often launched their midgets from naval basins or river estuaries, leaving the tiny craft to make their way across expanses of open ocean before reaching their targets, larger submarines usually towed the X-class subs close to their targets.

Only when very close did the X-craft's crew transfer over to their midget by boat and make the rest of the journey under their own power. This greatly reduced losses to bad weather or navigational errors as compared to the German K-Verband.

The most famous expedition by X-class midgets occurred in 1943 against the battleship KMS *Tirpitz*. A 43,000 ton giant similar to the famous KMS *Bismarck*, the *Tirpitz* lurked in the Scandinavian fjords, a place the British believed it immune to both air and surface attack. The British government viewed it as a menace to convoys as long as it remained afloat. Prime Minister Winston Churchill referred to it as "the Beast."

The *Tirpitz*

A plan to sink the *Tirpitz* using charges delivered by six X-craft – X5, X6, X7, X8, X9, and X10 – came together under the name "Operation Source" in autumn 1943. Half a dozen S-class and T-class submarines set out on September 11th, each towing one of the midget submarines. The strange convoy spent days sailing through Arctic waters towards the northern fjords of Norway. Along the way, X9 detached and sank, carrying a transit crew of three men to their deaths in the crushing blackness of the ocean depths. Shortly thereafter, mechanical failures forced the scuttling of X8.

Aerial reconnaissance and the Norwegian Resistance enabled the British to pinpoint the *Tirpitz* in Kaafjord, a limb of the larger Altenfjord. A Norwegian Resistance member, Torstein Raaby, rented a house overlooking Kaafjord, enabling him to ensure the *Tirpitz* remained in place.

The four remaining X-class midgets decoupled from the larger submarines on September 20th and proceeded to the fjord under their own power. The small craft slipped past the anti-submarine boom at the fjord entrance and slipped unharmed through a minefield before spending the night lurking near a small island, charging their batteries. Ship traffic picked up considerably after dark, though the commercial vessels felt safe enough to sail with running lights, giving the crews of the midgets an exact fix on their location to avoid sightings or collisions.

At 7 AM sharp the next morning, Lieutenant Donald Cameron, commanding X6, nicknamed the *Piker*, saw the Germans raising the boom at the entrance of Kaafjord to admit a small coastal patrol craft. Despite the brilliant sunlight and the mirror-like stillness of the fjord's surface, he immediately ordered the *Piker* to the surface. The X-craft followed the German coaster through into the inner fjord, then made straight for the *Tirpitz* just two miles away, sailing up the inlet with almost insouciant confidence.

The Germans spotted X6 just as it dived under their battleship. With considerable presence of mind, the men on deck immediately opened fire with machine guns, while hurling grenades and small depth charges over the side. Cameron ordered the 4,400 lb mines dropped as the tiny attacker slid under its giant quarry. The crew obeyed, but the sudden lightening caused the X6 to bob up violently, smashing into the *Tirpitz's* keel and suffering catastrophic damage.

Cameron and the rest of the X6's crew escaped the wreck. The Germans fished the bedraggled Englishmen out of the water and took them prisoner. At the same time, X7 under the command of Lieutenant George Place entered the fjord by sliding along the muddy bottom under the submarine nets. This vessel, unofficially nicknamed the *Pdinichthys*, deposited its charges also but suffered severe damage from German machine gun bullets. Forced to the surface, the X7 sustained more holes and the crew abandoned ship, though the firing killed two of them.

The Germans brought their British prisoners aboard the *Tirpitz* shortly before the charges on the bottom detonated. Cameron described what happened next: "Crash! My knees buckled as the explosion hurled the ship out of the water. [...] I was grabbed by the guard and pushed through the door into the bright sunlight. What a change in those few moments! The ship started to list rapidly to port. Steam rushed from broken pipes. Seamen raced in all directions. Oil flowed from the shattered hull covering the water of the fiord. Injured men were being brought up on deck." (Peillard, 1984, 240).

German boats coursed wildly up and down the fjord, dropping depth charges indiscriminately. X5 under Lieutenant Henty Henty-Creer vanished, probably destroyed with the loss of all hands by a depth charge. The Germans recovered a jumble of wreckage, but no corpses, from a spot near the shore several days later.

The X10, under Lieutenant Ken Hudspeth, suffered mechanical problems. The crew brought the X10 to rest on the seabed outside Kaafjord and spent hours trying to repair the midget sub. When they heard the explosions, however, they deemed correctly that the Germans would spend hours dropping depth charges and their chances of accomplishing anything with a malfunctioning X-craft approached nil. Accordingly, Hudspeth ordered the X10 taken back out to sea, jettisoning the two charges set to "safe" mode. The men met with HMS *Stubborn,* which retrieved them but found it necessary to scuttle X10 during a stormy trip back to Scotland.

The *Tirpitz* failed to sink, and the hull barely cracked, but the shock of the massive charges destroyed much of the vessel's engine machinery and caused its oil bunkers to leak. This immobilized the *Tirpitz* for 6 months, until repairs completed in March 1944, immediately before a Royal Air Force bombing decisively sank the vessel at anchor.

The X-class midget submarines continued to operate in very limited numbers throughout the war. X24 sank the *Barenfels,* an ammunition ship, off Bergen in 1944. During the D-Day landings in June 1944, two midgets, X-20 under Ken Hudspeth and X-23 under George Honour, served as marker ships for the invasion armada. The tiny subs moved ahead of the fleet, then surfaced and raised telescoping masts equipped with marker lights: "No sound or sign disturbed the air until, from seaward, there came a throbbing. [...] The assault forces were arriving. [...] There were twenty, thirty, forty ships in a column, stretching away out of sight. There were as many columns stretching away to port and starboard. And then there were the men. [...] [Lt. Honour] could see a few of them. A few more could see him. Most of them probably didn't know who X.23 was or what she had been doing, but they all gave a cheery wave." (Warren, 1954, 241).

American Operations in the Atlantic

The U.S. Navy participated in the Atlantic as a combatant, but it deployed only a few submarines to that theater. In all, six American submarines, including the famous USS *Barb* (credited with sinking the most tonnage of Japanese ships during the war) served in the Atlantic, but the Navy shifted all these vessels to the Pacific by the middle of 1943, at which point only U.S. submarines in transit from their shipyards to the Pacific Ocean passed through Atlantic waters.

The USS *Barb*

The detachment of American submarines in the Atlantic received the designation Submarine Squadron 50, or SubRon 50. Based in Rosneath, Scotland at a group of bleak Quonset huts, these far-ranging subs attempted to intercept Kriegsmarine U-boats, patrolled for Axis blockade runners, and assisted the Operation Torch landings in North Africa. The USS *Beaver* (AS-5), a repurposed passenger steamer originally built in 1910, served as SubRon 50's tender.

The USS *Beaver*

Both British and American submarines served as beacon ships during Operation Torch, lying at the surface with infrared signal lights to mark the landing points for the incoming troop transports. Five SubRon 50 vessels participated, working as beacons near Safi, Mehedia, and Fedhala. USS *Barb* under Lieutenant Commander John R. Waterman also put ashore five U.S. Army scouts in a rubber boat at Safi, to find landing points for General George Patton's tanks.

The beacon ship concept failed to work correctly, leading to chaotic landings under fire. However, the *Gato*-class USS *Herring* spotted the 5,700-ton Vichy French cargo vessel *Ville du Havre* and sank it with torpedoes. Simultaneously, the sixth SubRon 50 submarine, USS *Blackfish*, lurked outside Dakar harbor in case the Vichy ships there attempted a sortie against the Allied vessels executing Operation Torch, but the French stayed quiescent.

After the Torch landings and a period of repairs and refits at Rosneath, SubRon 50 patrolled off Spain's coast during late 1942 and early 1943, looking for Axis blockade runners. The submarines encountered many Spanish merchant vessels and swarms of fishing boats, but only once did USS *Barb* launch torpedoes, as Everett H. Steinmetz (later commander of the submarine USS *Crevalle* in the Pacific) reported: "The routine was broken one evening as we believed we had spotted a German tanker. A night surface attack was conducted and two hits were observed. Johnny Waterman, the Skipper swore he saw our victim's turbines blow clear of the superstructure. Spirits soared [...] However, immediately upon return to Rosneath, the Skipper was ordered to report to the Admiralty. After interrogation, he was informed the tanker was Spanish, not German." (Steinmetz, 1998, NA).

The Spanish tanker, despite damage, reached port, and Francisco Franco's government issued a vehement protest to the British. The Royal Navy eluded the issue by stating that whatever submarine attacked the tanker, it was certainly not British!

Soon, the Admiralty reassigned SubRon 50 to a subarctic patrol area, believing the battleship KMS *Tirpitz* planned a breakout into the Atlantic. After several weeks of fruitless patrols among ice floes, the submarines received yet another assignment searching for German "milch cow" refueling subs off the British coast. Due to poor coordination by the Admiralty, these efforts proved useless also, and the U.S. Navy withdrew the submarines to New London, Connecticut before reassigning them to the Pacific. This ended American submarine operations in the Atlantic.

While the half-dozen USN submarines assigned to the Atlantic failed to sink a single U-boat and did very little damage to Axis blockade runners, America's Navy contributed other assets to the Battle of the Atlantic. In the struggle against the packs of U-boats, the Anglo-American forces used any and all means at their disposal, including some 133 blimps cruising the skies above the Atlantic, shepherding convoys of supply ships, transports, and Liberty Ships and performing valuable scouting missions while conserving fuel.

The Americans' use of zeppelin escorts, the K-ships, to protect convoys and drop depth charges on attacking U-boats, remains little-known today. Nevertheless, the long, gleaming, neoprene-coated balloons of the K-ships slid through the Atlantic skies above many convoys between early 1942 and the end of the European war in 1945. During this time the zeppelins escorted some 70,000 surface ships and carried out numerous scouting expeditions during more than 37,000 individual sorties.

K-ships, built by Goodyear Aircraft Company and powered by a pair of Pratt & Whitney engines attached to propellers, measured around 250 feet long. Cruising at 58 miles per hour (though frequently matching the much slower speed of a surface convoy), these bloated, silvery airships could reach 78 miles per hour in an emergency. Each carried a .50 caliber machine gun for defense, alongside a rack of 350-lb depth charges.

Though the K-ships lacked sufficient room in their gondolas to take survivors of successful U-boat attacks on board, they still offered useful aid to such men. They reported the position of occupied lifeboats or individual sailors to craft capable of retrieving these survivors, and carried supplies of food and water they lowered to men in lifeboats, increasing their chances of survival markedly.

Enthusiastic K-ship crews frequently reported dropping their depth charges on enemy submarines, often confidently noting they had identified these as German or Italian based on clues known only to themselves. Regardless of their relative effectiveness, the zeppelins provided a unique morale boost to Allied seamen: "The men of the merchant marine [...] knew that, like their own vessels, surface escorts were vulnerable to underwater attack. The blimp was not. Airplanes, of course, were not vulnerable either, but they came and went in a hurry [...] The blimp stayed with the convoy, flying low and throttling back to keep a slow pace. [...] Airship crews and merchant ship crews waved to each other, the airship looking all the while majestic and overwhelmingly powerful and reassuring." (Vaeth, 1992, 68-69).

In fact, no confirmed record of a U.S. zeppelin sinking a U-boat exists, though the gleefully vigorous dropping of depth charges probably inflicted some unrecorded minor damage over the course of 4 years of war. Additional specialized types, such as the G-ship, the L-ship, and the M-ship joined the roster as the war progressed.

In addition to whatever damage they inflicted, the airships spotted many German submarines, directing other, faster-moving assets to the area and frequently prompting a retreat or causing the occasional kill. These American Goodyear zeppelins affected German morale as well; later U-boat survivor testimonies suggest that the packs of submarines hesitated to approach a convoy shadowed by the gleaming, oblong shape of a blimp, whose ongoing presence bespoke sleepless vigilance.

American airships achieved great popularity with the merchant crews and captains in the Atlantic convoys, with the presence of a blimp increasing the men's feeling of safety. The blimp offered a psychological boost neither destroyers nor fixed-wing aircraft emulated. Destroyers, moving on the surface, could also be sunk and therefore seemed fragile compared to the K-ships with their lofty perch in the sky, utterly immune to torpedoes. Regular aircraft remained for only a few minutes at most.

In turn, The blimp crews frequently developed highly protective feelings towards the ships they escorted. Lieutenant Commander James Cruse noted his distress when the Germans sank a tanker he picked out for protection, following a forced return to base due to exhausted fuel for the blimp's propellers. He described the ship as "one beautiful vessel [...] freshly painted, clean, and confidently plowing her way along [...] I couldn't help but admire her and I was determined no German was going to get this prize vessel while I was around. I flew coverage for her all day but at nightfall I had to return to Glynco [...] The next morning at the Squadron Operations Office I looked at the board. Listed was 'my ship,' call letters KOZT, with the word SUNK next to it. I was shocked. I felt I had lost a friend (Vaeth, 1992,   69-70).

Only on one occasion did one of the American blimps possibly sink a U-boat, though the sight of the airships frightened off many would-be attackers, generally causing an emergency crash dive when they appeared in the distance. On May 5th, 1945, Helmut Fromsdorfer's U-853, a snorkel-equipped Type IXC sub, sank SS *Black Point* just off the coast of Rhode Island in a daring late-war raid. K-ships K-16 and K-58 dropped buoys to track the U-boat, then a series of six depth charges. Surface ships also dropped depth charges.

A few moments after the last pair of blimp-launched depth charges exploded, a mass of wreckage spurted to surface, including wood fragments, life jackets, a mattress, and a German naval officer's hat. U-853 sank with all hands, though whether due to the bombs from the blimps, the surface ships, or both could not be determined.

Grand Admiral Karl Dönitz himself provided an opinion on the effect of America's airship squadrons on Atlantic submarine warfare: "It is possible that a U-boat commander, at the sight of a 'blimp' might conclude that a convoy was nearby. On the other hand, there was also the possibility that the sighted 'blimp' was only on patrol. But even if the commander, upon seeing the 'blimp,' surmised a convoy, that would only be a slight disadvantage to the use of a 'blimp' since it would hinder the U-boat's approach, at the very least severely ." (Vaeth, 1992, 172).

Dönitz

The role of the American blimps in submarine warfare remained chiefly psychological, from both sides' viewpoints. Nevertheless, even the deterrent threat of a blimp seriously impeded U-boat operations, since the airships escorted no less than 70,000 Allied vessels during the war.

A final ingredient in the American contribution to Atlantic submarine warfare consisted of the *Bogue*-class escort carriers, a far more lethal anti-submarine weapons system than the K-ships, L-ships, or ZP-ships. Made from modified merchant ships, these small carriers featured decks 496 feet long and 111 feet wide, with a small bridge attached for spotting, navigation, and communications.

A *Bogue*-class escort carrier

Unusually, these anti-submarine carriers drew power from a pair of Foster Wheeler steam boilers providing a cruising speed of 19 mph, rather than the diesel engines used in many other carrier classes. Thus, the Bogue-class ships remained actual steamships in an era of petroleum powered vessels. Each carrier featured either or one or two catapults and a complement of tough Navy aircraft: "The catapult equipment and machinery was housed in the number one cargo hold. Configured as an aircraft transport, the BOGUE class could accommodate fifty   aircraft on the flight deck and forty below on the hangar deck. For normal flight   operations, up to twenty-four aircraft could be handled, normally split twelve F4F (FM) Wildcat fighters and twelve TBF (TBM) torpedo bombers in a composite squadron." (Squadron/Signal, 1996, 9).

While the Navy dispatched some Bogue-class carriers to the Pacific, the eponymous USS *Bogue* (originally *Steel Advocate*) plus USS *Block Island, Card, Core,* and *Croatan* remained in the Atlantic until Germany's surrender, fighting Dönitz's U-boats. USS *Bogue* and its escorts ultimately sank 13 U-boats, while USS *Card* destroyed 8 Axis submarines. The crews painted the outline of a submarine with a Nazi flag superimposed over it onto the outer surface of the bridge for each confirmed U-boat kill. Both *Bogue* and *Card* received the Presidential Unit Citation.

One of USS *Card's* first successes showed the dramatic successes these small carriers sometimes enjoyed. On October 4th, 1943, a radar contact showed a group of U-boats at the surface north of the Azores. Wildcats and Avengers screamed into the air off *Card's* wooden flight deck and caught four German U-boats at the surface, three of them refueling from a fourth "milch cow" variant. Dropping depth charges on the rapidly scattering U-boats, the aircraft destroyed the U-460, leaving only two survivors. Shortly afterward, the Avengers launched Mark 24 Fido acoustic homing torpedoes, sinking U-422 and killing the submarine's entire crew. Neither of the U-boats had yet succeeded in sinking any Allied vessels.

A month later, on November 1st, one of *Card's* escorts, the *Clemson*-class destroyer USS *Borie*, sank Rolf-Heinrich Hopmann's U-405. In a dramatic action, *Borie* first depth-charged U-405, damaging its hull sufficiently to force the submarine to flee on the surface. *Borie* pursued the U-boat through a violent storm, finally ramming the German vessel and finishing it off with a fusillade of small arms fire loosed from the destroyer's deck. The ramming attack inflicted fatal damage to the *Borie* also – the ship sank with the loss of 27 hands, while 130 men survived thanks to rescue by other destroyers.

The USS *Borie*

While the *Bogue*-class escort carriers proved their worth in anti-submarine warfare, the Germans responded aggressively to their presence. Wolf-Pack Borkum, a swarm of no less than 17 U-boats, launched a relentless series of attacks against USS *Card* and its escorts during the night of December 23rd-24th, 1943, 585 miles west of Cape Finesterre. U-415 came closest to sinking the escort carrier at 1:43 a.m., when it launched a trio of torpedoes *Card* eluded by only a few yards.

The Borkum U-boats persisted in their attacks for hours, torpedoing USS *Leary* and causing a massive internal explosion that killed 97 men, including Commander James Kyes. USS *Schenck* rescued the 59 survivors, sinking the lurking U-648 shortly after dodging one of the U-boat's torpedoes. U-415 sank the British destroyer HMS *Hurricane* 18 hours later as the *Card* task group and Wolf-Pack Borkum continued to stalk each other over the lonely expanses of the central Atlantic.

A bold U-boat skipper, the 26 year old Danzig native Detlev Krankenhagen, inflicted the only escort carrier loss to a submarine to occur in the Atlantic, on May 29th, 1944. Krankenhagen – a boyish-looking, blond-haired individual with deep-set, intense eyes – and his crew spotted the *Bogue*-class USS *Block Island,* ringed by a screen of destroyers, sailing westward southwest of Madeira under an overcast sky with occasional frontal rain. U-549 slipped past the destroyers and fired three torpedoes at *Block Island.*

Captain Francis Massie Huges described the moment of the attack, which caught the vessel completely unawares: "Without warning of any kind, a torpedo struck BLOCK ISLAND forward. [...] Approximately three seconds later, a second torpedo struck the ship with a shattering explosion. I made my way to the bridge as quickly as possible. Enroute I noticed the port side of the flight deck curled back about ten feet and the forward part of the flight deck covered with oily water. I noticed the general condition of the ship and knew we had been pretty badly hurt." (Huges, 1944, 6).

The *Bogue*-class carrier settled rapidly by the stern while the efficient Huges organized his men to abandon ship. Only 10 sailors died thanks both to the location of the hits and the calm professionalism of the officers and crew. Huges considered dumping the aircraft overboard to slow the sinking, but decided against it as their ruptured gas tanks could create a burning slick on the water surface. He also sped up the process of abandoning ship due to the chance of another torpedo detonating the 135 depth charges and 65,000 gallons of aviation gasoline carried on board the *Block Island* – capable of creating a vast explosion likely to kill every man still aboard the doomed vessel.

951 officers and crew survived to be rescued from the water by the destroyers. Chief Carpenter Clarence Bailey refused to leave the ship due to a man with his leg trapped between the forward catwalk and the ship's main structure. Bailey and two pharmacist's mates remained on the *Block Island* for an hour as it slowly sank, trying desperately to free the sailor by cutting away pieces of the catwalk with an acetylene torch. Finally, unable to work his leg free, they amputated the man's leg at the knee with a sheath knife, which freed him but proved fatal as he died within a few moments from shock and blood loss.

Huges himself left the ship last, leaping into the water and swimming to a small boat some distance away. While the destroyers' boats worked to pick up the hundreds of men still in the water, the depth charges aboard *Block Island* started detonating as an internal fire reached them. Suddenly, a giant blast rolled through the ocean as the depth charges set off *Block Island*'s torpedo magazine, making the crew of a nearby destroyer believe a torpedo struck their ship. The escort carrier tipped up vertically on end and plunged out of sight into the depths of the ocean.

Krankenhagen had little time to enjoy his victory. Instead of trying to escape, U-549 turned on the destroyers, damaging the USS *Barr* with another torpedo strike, then stalking *Ahrens*. Loitering on the scene proved fatal. The destroyer USS *Eugene E. Elmore,* under the command of George Conkey, zeroed in on the U-boat and shattered it with depth charges. Every man aboard died as the water pressure and blasts caved in U-549's hull.

The Heyday of U-Boats in the Atlantic

When the United Kingdom and France declared war on the Third Reich following its September 1939 invasion of Poland, the initial phase of the conflict gained the sobriquet of the "Phoney War" due to French and British inaction against Germany's western frontier. Other than a feeble French incursion into the Saar region, soon withdrawn, the western Allies failed to attack the Third Reich while its armies remained busy in the east.

In the maritime theater, however, the Phoney War proved quite violent. Just as the Pearl Harbor assault began with an abortive Japanese midget submarine attack, submarines opened the hostilities between Britain and Germany in the Atlantic.

The Kriegsmarine remained scarcely influenced by Nazi ideology throughout the war, instead displaying naval professionalism characteristic of the German navy for generations. Though brave, patriotic, and skilled, the sailors and commanders of the U-boats showed little fanaticism, instead often exhibiting chivalric tendencies, especially early in the war.

Hitler himself, wanting to keep the British amenable to peace in the near future and keen to avoid infuriating the United States, issued extremely restrictive rules about acceptable U-boat targets. These rules excluded basically any non-British vessel except French ships in convoys or directly engaged in hostile operations, while exempting British passenger ships from attack.

However, much to the horror of the Fuhrer, Admiral Karl Dönitz, and Friedrich-Julius Lemp (the U-boat commander involved), the first submarine "kill" of the war violated every one of the Kriegsmarine's and Hitler's remarkably civilized strictures. Lemp led U-30 in a mistaken dusk attack on the ocean liner *SS Athenia,* killing 118 passengers, including 28 American civilians. Lemp increased the problems by guiltily fleeing the scene, failing to inform his superiors of the error or trying to help the stricken ship. Dönitz and Hitler learned of this diplomatic catastrophe only when a hurricane of deep moral outrage broke out among their enemies.

Lemp and Dönitz

Despite Hitler's qualms, submarine warfare necessarily involved ambush predator tactics contravening the laws of war as laid down prior to the creation of underwater vessels. Unable to fight with any hope of success against the massed guns of a surface warship, submarines needed to strike without warning and, generally, abandon the crews of the stricken ships to their fate as they made their escape underwater.

To be fair, the Americans and British used precisely the same tactics against Axis shipping, including the merchant marine, as the U-boats used against Allied merchant and military craft. Indeed, specifically and explicitly for this reason, the victorious Western Allies brought no war crimes charges against any Kriegsmarine personnel for sinking merchant ships after the war's end. Only those few individuals who committed obvious atrocities, such as shooting lifeboats or people left floating helplessly in the water, found themselves arraigned for crimes against humanity.

The Kriegsmarine, in fact, often showed a degree of chivalric punctilio somewhat unexpected in a 20th century war. Atrocities occurred among the submarine services of the Germans, British, and Americans alike, but they remained the exception rather than the rule. Only the Imperial Japanese Navy's submarine service produced an extraordinary number of war criminals, participating in torture, massacres of prisoners, and, in cases where female civilians or personnel fell into their hands, frequent, unpunished rape.

Within a few days of Lemp drawing first blood, the U-boats began sinking a number of British merchant vessels on the Atlantic, and other U-boats carried out the difficult task of precision minelaying in channels frequented by the Allied merchant marine. At this point in the war, unless attacked immediately by escorts, the U-boats often stopped to assist survivors with their lifeboats. Some captains also radioed rescue information to the opposing naval forces, a practice often repeated throughout the war in the Atlantic and Mediterranean by both sides when a captain found himself obliged to leave a number of survivors in the water. Herbert Schultze's *U-48* sank the freighter *Firby* on September 11th, 1939, after which the U-boat's doctor bandaged several wounded British sailors and the Germans placed food and water on board the *Firby's* lifeboats. Schultze then broadcast an uncoded radio signal: "Transmit to Mr. Churchill. I have sunk the British steamer *Firby*. Posit fifty-nine degrees forty minutes north, thirteen degrees fifty minutes west. Save the crew if you please. German submarine." (Blair, 1996, 152).

The British did not remain passive in the face of this challenge but attempted to strike back. Skua aircraft from the famous aircraft carrier *Ark Royal* located Lemp's *U-30* on September 14th and attempted to bomb the submarine. However, their poorly designed bombs actually bounced back from the water surface and exploded in midair, inadvertently bringing down two of the Skuas. The Germans gallantly halted and rescued the two pilots, despite machine gun fire from other Skuas, and later set the men ashore on neutral Iceland.

The *Ark Royal* in 1939

U-39, skippered by Gerhard Glattes, stalked *Ark Royal* while this drama unfolded elsewhere. *Ark Royal*'s destroyers had steamed ahead while the aircraft carrier launched its Skuas. Glattes' crew fired a spread of torpedoes, but due to faulty magnetic pistols, all detonated before reaching the ship's hull. The destroyers returned in haste at reports of torpedo detonations near the *Ark Royal* and pummeled *U-39* with depth charges. When his U-boat sustained moderate damage, Glattes panicked, ordered the submarine to surface, and told his men to abandon ship. The U-boat's scuttling charge went off, sinking the vessel, and the British successfully rescued the entire 43-man crew from the waves, winning the war's first anti-submarine victory.

A Type IXA submarine, the U-39's class

The U-boats continued to pounce on British tankers and merchantmen, though not on the scale they would develop later in the war. On October 14th, however, Gunther Prien and the crew of *U-47* executed a raid of exceptional daring against the main British fleet base at the remote Orkney Islands location of Scapa Flow. Prien brought his submarine into the unprepared harbor late at night, under a starry sky filled with the ghostly flashes of Aurora borealis. The U-boat cautiously avoided a patrolling destroyer and bypassed the inadequate line of blockships at the harbor entrance. The British had permitted Scapa Flow's defenses to deteriorate seriously between the wars, and Prien experienced little difficulty slipping inside.

Once inside, Prien torpedoed the battleship HMS *Royal Oak*, sinking it and killing at least 786 men, including Admiral Henry Blagrove, who quietly refused to leave the vessel. Some casualty figures range as high as 883 deaths. Prien used the tactic of spinning his submarine to fire alternately with the prow and stern torpedo tubes, and it was the third salvo that destroyed *Royal Oak*.

Upon learning the particulars of the attack, Winston Churchill made two remarks. About the crew of the *Royal Oak,* many of whom survived the initial attack only to die by inches of asphyxiation inside the overturned hull, he stated, "Poor fellows, poor fellows, trapped in those black depths." (Turner, 2008, 52). However, he also described the U-boat attack as "a wonderful feat of arms," encapsulating war's contrast between incredible achievements of courage, endurance, ingenuity, and horror.

The *Royal Oak*

Though destroyers finally launched to pursue the retreating U-boat, Prien made his escape by choosing a route very close to the shore. The long, low, slick black hull of his submarine twice came under the glare of spotlights, and the headlights of a vehicle on shore illuminated it once, but every time, the British failed to identify his craft for what it was and the daring German crew lived to fight another day.

Though both sides knew the group tactics they intended to use – wolf-packs on the German side and convoys on the Allied side – neither employed these methods initially. During 1939 and 1940 the U-boats continued operating singly, while the Allies used few convoys during the same period. Only in 1941 did convoys and wolf-packs appear as common tactical arrangements.

U-boat operations in the Atlantic remained fairly limited until 1940, when the conquest of France in May through June provided the Third Reich with a massive windfall of new port facilities. Rather than being limited to launching U-boats from the short German coast and negotiating the narrow straits between Denmark and Scandinavia to reach the open waters of the Atlantic, the Kriegsmarine now built U-boat pens at five major locations along the French coast.

Though superbly located adjacent to British territorial waters, these new bases also lay a very short distance from airfields in England. Royal Air Force (RAF) bombing attacks could occur at any time. Accordingly, the Germans constructed massively fortified, highly sophisticated U-boat bases capable of withstanding heavy, prolonged bombing.

The new bases included Brest, Lorient, St. Nazaire, La Pallice, and Bordeaux. At each location, the Germans constructed huge concrete bunkers housing multiple flooded U-boat pens. The engineers designed many of these pens to be closed, then pumped dry, allowing access to the entire hull for repair crews. As the war went on, construction of additional "drydock pens" became a priority, to repair U-boats damaged in action and return them to service as rapidly as possible.

An extensive complex attached to each bunker, including workshops, repair facilities, fuel depots, ammunition dumps, cranes and turntables capable of lifting and moving an entire U-boat, barracks for crews and shore personnel, and many other facilities. The Germans built these bunkers so solidly that they survived numerous bombing raids essentially undamaged, as well as postwar weathering and civilian activity. Most remain in an excellent state of preservation at the start of the 21st century. In fact, the French navy took over many of these excellent facilities following World War II's end.

Late in 1939, the S-class submarine HMS *Salmon* struck back with some effect against the Kriegsmarine near Norway. On December 4th, *Salmon* observed *U-36* at the surface near Stavenger, and successfully ambushed the German sub, sinking it with a loss of all hands using a single torpedo. Later on the same patrol, *Salmon* severely damaged the light cruiser *Leipzig* and inflicted moderate damage on the light cruiser *Nurnberg*.

The HMS *Salmon*

British submarines attempted to intercept the invasion force sent to Norway, since the Luftwaffe and Kriegsmarine controlled the seas between Germany and Scandinavia too effectively in 1940 for the RN or RAF to halt the attack. However, the Germans enjoyed the fruits of an intelligence coup of their own. German Abwehr (military intelligence) personnel detected the radio signals of the handful of British submarines operating in the area, and neatly steered the invasion flotilla clear of them.

The British also used submarines in the Mediterranean against Italian naval forces in the process of shipping supplies, vehicles, and men to the North African theater. In 1940, these submarines sank only a few vessels while suffering relatively heavy losses. However, strong reinforcements in 1941 bolstered the success of Royal Navy submarines operating from Malta. The tactical skills of the new regional commander, G.W.G. "Shrimp" Simpson, also boosted the submarine success rate.

In 1940, German submarines laid numerous mines in main shipping channels near Britain. As a deliberate strategy, the U-boats struck chiefly at neutral rather than British merchant ships sailing to England. The intent was to deter other nations from assisting the embattled UK.

1940 also brought to light problems with the U-boats' torpedoes. Faulty magnetic pistols or "exploders" as sometimes known caused many torpedoes to detonate prematurely. This caused several months of "down time" as the technicians hurriedly refitted all torpedoes with contact detonators, which ensured only actual hits would cause an explosion, but required greater accuracy in use.

The new detonators paid dividends and late in 1940 Dönitz expressed his satisfaction: "If even two days passed without my receiving reports of ships having been sighted by U-boats I at once ordered a redistribution of my forces. As it became more and more evident that we stood an excellent chance of achieving really great successes, I was most anxious that not one single day should pass without the sinking somewhere or other of a ship by one of the boats at sea." (Hoyt, 1984, 61).

The combination of new access to French ports and bases, plus the new torpedo arrangements, ushered in the "First Happy Time" – a period of marked success for the U-boats. Additionally, the British ships very seldom had radar, and since the prowling U-boats struck at night on the surface, it made them all but invisible to the ASDIC used by the convoys at that time. The First Happy Time lasted from June to October of 1940 and witnessed the sinking of 282 ships, totaling just short of 1.5 million tons.

However, German submarines weren't the only ones enjoying success. In the first quarter of 1941 alone, the British submarines sank 150,000 tons of Axis shipping plying the waters between Italy and North Africa. The Germans responded by sending U-boats, E-boats (fast, torpedo-armed patrol and attack motorboats), and sonar sets for the Italians to mount on their anti-submarine destroyers. By early 1942, these countermeasures contributed to the sinking of a number of Royal Navy submarines. The Germans and Italians laid extensive minefields around Malta also, which sank nearly as many submarines as the U-boats and Italian ships. By March to April 1942, the British decided to abandon Malta as a submarine base. Though the Axis lost 117,000 tons of merchant shipping to the undaunted submarine crews, 94% of the supplies needed by the Afrika Korps and Italian forces still arrived safely.

By July 1942, the British established a new submarine base at Gibraltar and replaced their losses. This submarine force assisted the October invasion of North Africa by a fresh Anglo-American force, Operation Torch. Over the following months, 32 Royal Navy submarines pounded Axis convoys in conjunction with heavy air attacks. The aircraft ultimately claimed more shipping, but the submarines did their part in choking off the Axis resupply effort. The lack of supplies and reinforcements contributed strongly to the surrender of the last Afrika Korps forces in Tunisia in late spring 1943.

The British lost only 1 submarine to U-boats, while sinking 19 of their Axis counterparts in the Mediterranean. Despite the excellence of U-boat crew training, the English quickly developed superior tactics tailored to the Mediterranean's idiosyncrasies: " British submarines [...] remained submerged in daylight, not only in the patrol zones, but in transit [...] The radio was used as sparingly as possible because of the accurate Axis radio direction finding stations [...] a 'porpoising' strategy was said to have been developed, whereby every quarter hour the submarine came up for anall- round view (especially for aircraft) before submerging into the depths again." (McCartney, 2008, 39-40).

The relatively limited size of the Mediterranean made submerged travel a viable tactic. The Kriegsmarine U-boats, accustomed to the vast spaces of the Atlantic, traveled on the surface for speed, only submerging once enemy surface vessels or aircraft appeared. This explains the imbalance in losses between the rival submarine forces. A U-boat's first warning that a British submarine operated nearby while it cruised incautiously on the surface usually consisted of a spread of torpedoes blowing its hull to pieces.

The entry of the United States into the war in December 1941 proved a brief but definite boon for the U-boat captains. Removal of the need to avoid antagonizing the Americans opened a huge new "hunting ground" to the Kriegsmarine subs. Like prey animals in a previously isolated habitat, the US Navy showed remarkable naivete it dealing with this new "predator." Initially, the USN eschewed convoys in favor of a more "offensive" approach.

The American rejection of convoys presented the U-boat captains with a smorgasbord of vulnerable ships. Though the Kriegsmarine only assigned 5 U-boats to American coastal waters and the Caribbean initially, this number soon mushroomed to 20. Presented with swarms of isolated, vulnerable ships, the U-boat skippers sank hundreds in short order. This "window" lasted only a relatively brief time, however, as the USN soon realized their lethal error and hastily adopted the convoy system.

Before that point, however, the Germans had much to be happy about. The Second Happy Time stretched from January-August 1942, proving more fruitful than the First. The U-boats claimed 609 ships in American waters, totaling 3.1 million tons. The Americans' failure to employ convoys also stemmed not only from senior USN overconfidence, but from a lack of sufficient escort ships. In such circumstances, the Navy felt it best to send out large numbers of individual ships rather than gathering them together in convoys they could not realistically defend. Nevertheless, Admiral Ernest King shares some responsibility for failing to develop American convoy capabilities sooner, largely due to his almost obsessive fixation on the Pacific campaign.

Adding further to the nexus of problems faced by the Allies during the Second Happy Time, the Kriegsmarine adopted a new Enigma coding machine, TRITON, early in 1942, making their signals temporarily impenetrable to the Allied codebreakers. It is perhaps significant that the Second Happy Time ended at the same time as the Allies captured TRITON code books from *U-559* in the waters off Egypt.

U-559, skippered by Hans-Otto Heidtmann, found itself in serious trouble on October 30th, 1942. Hunted relentlessly for much of the day after being discovered by a group of five British destroyers, the Germans finally surfaced at 10:40 PM after a depth charge compromised their hull.

Heidtmann hoped to escape in the darkness, but HMS *Hurworth* and *Petard* instantly spotted the U-boat and raked it with shattering gales of 40mm cannon fire. Heidtmann and several other men died, and the rest leapt overboard – an effective admission of surrender. Though the scuttling charge detonated, the crew neglected to destroy their Enigma machine separately in their panic.

Three brave volunteers entered the slowly sinking U-boat – Lieutenant Francis Fasson, Able Seaman Colin Grazier, and Canteen Assistant Thomas Brown, then a teenager technically too young to participate. Fasson, naked except for a flashlight and a machine gun, traversed U-559, soon sending Brown up to the deck with a stack of code books. While Fasson and Grazier tried to manhandle the Enigma machine up the conning tower ladder, the U-boat sank abruptly, sucking both men down to their deaths in the black waters of the midnight Mediterranean.

However, Brown and the code books reached a nearby whaleboat and from there got back aboard the destroyer. With the code books and careless errors on the part of Enigma operators, the Bletchley Park codebreakers and the British computing genius Alan Turing cracked the TRITON code in December. First Sea Lord Alfred Pound provided the codes to the

Americans, with a sneering note to Admiral Ernest J. King which, considering the latter's temper (Franklin D. Roosevelt once quipped that King "must shave with a blowTorch), likely produced more anger than appreciation: "You will, I am sure, appreciate the care necessary in making use of this information to prevent suspicion being aroused as to its source. We have found this especially difficult when action by [ship] routing authorities outside the Admiralty is required. It would be a tragedy if we had to start all over again on what would undoubtedly be a still more difficult problem." (Blair, 1998, 87).

Regardless of Pound's reservations, and the fury they doubtless awakened in the explosive, thorny King, the TRITON code break resulted in a rapid drop in ship losses in the early months of 1943. The time had nearly arrived for the pendulum of war's fortunes to swing in the opposite direction and the U-boats to suffer a very "unhappy" time.

Around the same time, Operation Husky, the Allied invasion of Sicily, constituted a highly successful swansong for a large British submarine presence in the Mediterranean. The submarines performed critical scouting duties, including putting stealthy parties of scouts and engineers ashore to observe the suitability of various beaches for assault. Once the Allies completed the conquest of Sicily and the bulk of Italy officially changed sides with the ousting of strongman Benito Mussolini from power, the British transferred most of their submarines to the Pacific and Indian Oceans to fight the Imperial Japanese Navy.

Allied Victory in the Atlantic

U-boat loss figures for the various war years provide a stark, objective picture of abrupt change in fortunes suffered by the German submarines in 1943. In 1939, 1940, and 1941, the Germans lost 9, 22, and 35 U-boats respectively. 1942, a transitional year, witnessed the sinking of 96 U-boats. A catastrophic jump in losses appears in 1943, however, with 237 "iron coffins" lost. The Allies sank a further 241 craft in 1944 and a blistering 153 U-boats in the first 5 months of 1945, theoretically annualizing to 367 if the war had continued the whole year.

Multiple factors converged to turn the Battle of the Atlantic decisively in the Allies' favor in early 1943. American production of destroyers, in their massive, bombing-free manufacturing facilities, finally reached its potential, making large numbers of high quality ships available for both escort and hunter-killer duties. The deployment of the escort carriers, such as the *Bogue*-class vessels, also inflicted losses on the U-boats, eliminating the mid-Atlantic area where air patrols were formerly impossible.

It's fair to say the Allies won the Battle of the Atlantic in April-May 1943, a period known as "Black May" to the U-boat crews. Air power formed the key element in the reversal, aided by centimetric radar, an invention which enabled fitting a small but powerful radar device into every anti-submarine aircraft and surface vessel, rather than just a select few. The Bay of Biscay became a hunting ground for Allied aircraft and a deep-water graveyard for the

Kriegsmarine.

In "Black May," the Allies sank 56 U-boats with the aid of new air cover and centrimetric radar. As late as May 19th, Dönitz remained in a shocking state of denial, issuing the following statement: "If there is anyone who thinks that fighting convoys is no longer possible, he is a weakling and no real U-boat commander. The Battle of the Atlantic gets harder but it is the decisive campaign of the war. Be aware of your high responsibility and be clear that you must answer for your actions.... Be hard, draw ahead, and attack. I believe in you. C-in-C." (Budiansky, 2013, 218).

Just four days later, the Grand Admiral realized his own folly and ordered the U-boats to withdraw, noting that each 10,000 tons of shipping sunk now cost a U-boat, in contrast to the Second Happy Time's "exchange rate" of one U-boat per 100,000 tons sunk. As a final blow to the U-boats, King ordered a new codebook introduced, which shut the Third Reich's codebreakers out of convoy communications for the rest of the war.

As U-boats continued to perish at a spiraling rate, Admiral Karl Donitz ordered the submarines to abandon the Atlantic struggle on May 24th, 1943. Though he lied to Hitler and stated the offensive would resume in a few weeks, the Admiral knew the Kriegsmarine had lost to the Anglo-American forces. The U-boats only sank 92 ships over the entire year between Donitz's retreat and the D-Day landings in June 1944.

In fact, plans for the D-Day landings would begin almost immediately after the Allied commanders realized the U-boats turned tail. Carriers such as the USS *Bogue* continued combing the Atlantic waters for intruders, but the days of the commerce raiders had ended. American Admiral Ernest J. King and British Admiral Sir Max Horton collaborated on developing a grand naval strategy during 1942, into 1943, and onward, which led to victory at sea and eventually on the European continent also.

The devastation of the U-boat forces in early to mid-1943 sent a clear signal to the Kriegsmarine and to Adolf Hitler in particular that these essential tools of maritime warfare needed revitalizing. The Type VII and IX U-boats could no longer function effectively in the naval warfare that evolved in Europe at this time.

Hitler, who varied between penetrating military insight and glaringly poor decisions in dealing with the war situation, recognized this need with his orders: "[I]n July Hitler gave high priority to the construction of completely new classes of submarines, most famously the type XXI. These new vessels represented a great leap forward in submarine design and were far superior to Allied vessels. They were built with streamlined hulls that allowed them to reach 18 knots under water and they had snorkels so that they could recharge their batteries and take in oxygen while submerged." (O'Brien, 2015, 25).

The Germans tried various technologies in addition to the snorkel boats, including radar detectors, increased flak armament on U-boats, and a variety of decoys. None stemmed the rapid bleeding of Kriegsmarine submarine strength or effectively countered the Allied technologies and tactics. The U-boats faded away as a significant strategic threat, instead becoming a weapon of occasional random terror and revenge.

In early May 1945, the 24-year-old skipper Hans Schaffer took his submarine, U-977, on a journey of epic misery to Argentina. This escape to South America from the doomed Third Reich spawned a flurry of books and articles positing that the vessel carried Adolf Hitler and Eva Braun, or perhaps their mortal remains, into exile. No evidence supports this fantastic claim, though Schaffer claimed an almost equally bizarre motive for the voyage: "One of my main reasons in deciding to proceed to the Argentine [...] was based on German propaganda which claimed that the American and British newspapers advocated... that all German men be enslaved and sterilized... It was absolutely my intention to deliver the boat undamaged into Allied hands, while doing the best I could for my crew. I felt the ship's engines might be a valuable adjunct to the reconstruction of Europe." (Blair, 1998, 675).

Even without Hitler, Braun, Martin Bormann, or any other leading Nazi aboard, U-977's voyage represented a notable feat of seamanship and applied technology. Despite previous damage from collisions with other German vessels and an accidental grounding off Norway, Schaffer's U-boat stayed underwater for 66 days between May 10th and July 14th, 1945, nearly driving his crew to mutiny or insanity due to the intolerable conditions on board. The ship finally surfaced in the tropics to allow the men some time to swim and clean themselves before moving on to Argentina.

Only one other U-boat escaped to South America. Several hundred skippers scuttled their submarines before surrendering, and 174 surrendered their boats intact. Of these, the British scuttled the majority either close to their current anchorage or off the northern coast of Ireland in an action known as Operation Deadlight.

A picture of dozens of U-boats moored off the coast during Operation Deadlight

Once the U-boat menace subsided and the Germans lost the capacity to build a powerful surface fleet, the European war's conclusion became foreordained. Neither the British nor the Soviets would succumb with the tremendous support offered by the industrial complexes and vast interior farmlands of the United States. As the Allies cemented control of the skies, the Germans increasingly suffered the same fate they inflicted on the Poles in the first days of the war. The Allies bombed factories, destroyed new tanks and vehicles in crippling numbers before the Germans managed to bring them into action, and cut off almost all large-scale transport of vital supplies and fuel.

Eventually, the Anglo-American air forces denied the Germans even local tactical movement, annihilating panzer or mechanized units from the air if they sought to move during the day. Even the famous Ardennes Offensive occurred in foul weather, crashing to a halt immediately when skies cleared and the flights of Spitfires, Mustangs, and Hellcats once again scoured the landscape like steel eagles watching keenly for prey.

In all, World War II's Atlantic theater witnessed strategically significant events in the struggle between Dönitz's U-boats and the combined forces of the western Allies. Carried out on the planet's second-largest single battlefield (the largest consisting of the Pacific Ocean), the submarine war in the Atlantic developed in precisely the opposite manner to that occurring on the other side of the globe.

In the Pacific, American submarines utterly devastated Japan's merchant marine, crippling the Imperial economy. They also wiped out a sizable portion of the IJN surface fleet, though less than the aircraft carriers and their lethal cargo of highly effective aircraft claimed. Despite representing only 2% of American fleet assets in the Pacific, the submarines proved a decisive weapons system thanks to the Japanese failure to develop either tactics or technology to counter them.

In the Atlantic, the story proved the opposite. Hitler and Dönitz hoped the U-boats would devastate Allied shipping in the same manner as the Americans eventually shredded Japan's merchant marine, but this dream never came close to fruition. The U-boat attacks caused chaos, devastation, and terror, but failed to choke Britain's wartime economy or even seriously threaten to halt the tide of Liberty Ships soon issuing from America's shores.

The Kriegsmarine men in the U-boat service had scant Nazi allegiance, instead fighting for age-old reasons of military professionalism, martial pride, and patriotism. Like their opposite numbers in the Allied navies, they showed immense courage and resourcefulness in a harsh, unforgiving battleground. More than 28,000 of these men died during the course of the war, and of 842 U-boats built and launched, the Allies sank 793, indicating both the determination of the German crews and the thoroughness of their defeat.

Despite the destruction, U-boats received a considerable portion of German industrial and ammunition production, ranging from over 11% in 1941 and 1942, dropping to 6.1% in 1943 as the factories retooled for the new Type XXI submarines and other snorkel-equipped U-boats, and rising to 8% again by 1944. Hitler's priority directives ranked U-boats and advanced fighter aircraft as the most urgent vehicles for manufacture, while Panzers disappeared entirely from factory priority lists by the late war period.

U-boats inflicted more damage on Allied shipping than any other method. Surface raiders and aircraft sank 30% of the ships lost to Axis attacks, while the submarines destroyed 70%. In total, the U-boats sank more than 3,000 vessels totaling over 14 million tons of shipping. The figures also provide a startling confirmation of individual aptitude's crucial role; just 3% of U-boat captains accounted for 28.6% of the total tonnage sunk (Williamson, 2005, 195).

The U-boat campaign had a significant morale effect on the Allies in addition to its practical constriction of British supplies. As Winston Churchill exclaimed, "How willingly would I have exchanged a full-scale attempt at invasion for this shapeless, measureless peril, expressed in charts, curves, and statistics!" (Budiansky, 2013, 132-133).

The submarine had an important future before it as a nuclear-powered vessel during the Cold War, able to hold the threat of nuclear destruction out of reach of conventional strikes. The use of submarines in the Atlantic during World War II, however, demonstrated the limitations as well as the possibilities of this stealthy weapons system. The Americans had the good fortune to use their Pacific submarines as part of a combined-arms strategy, and they succeeded, whereas the Germans, limited by many factors, tried to use the submarine as a completely independent weapon, inflicted considerable losses on their adversaries, and ultimately failed, all at a bitter cost to the brave men who piloted "Hitler's canoes" against the Allies.

Submarine Warfare in the Pacific

Submarine Warfare at Pearl Harbor

On the morning of December 7th, 1941, calm and beautiful weather lay over the land and sea surrounding Pearl Harbor on the island of Oahu. A delicate mist, touched with color by the dawn, floated above the smooth blue surface of the sea, while the hills of the island glowed green with foliage. Japanese bombs soon shattered the peace of this pleasant Sunday morning, plunging the United States headlong into World War II and bringing the U.S. Navy (USN) and Marine Corps into action across the far-flung Pacific Theater in a bitterly fought and dramatic campaign.

The first shot of this engagement did not involve aircraft, however. Somewhat earlier, at around 4 AM, a somewhat ungainly USN minesweeper, the *USS Condor*, spotted a pale streak of foam crossing the dim predawn waters outside the harbor. Interpreting this correctly as the track of a submarine periscope, the *Condor*'s commander radioed the sighting, along with speed and direction, to the destroyer *USS Ward*, Lieutenant William Outerbridge commanding.

A Lapwing-class Minesweeper

While the *Condor* retired into the harbor, the *Ward* moved to investigate. Outerbridge did not know that five Imperial Japanese Navy (IJN) Type A midget submarines prowled the waters nearby; the one spotted by *Condor* surfaced due to mechanical troubles. Yamamoto did not want the midget submarines on the mission because they might be seen prior to the air attack – precisely what actually happened. However, other men badgered him into accepting the small undersea vessels' presence.

Five larger submarines, with the identifying numbers I-16, I-18, I-20, I-22, and I-24, moved close to Oahu early on the morning of December 7th and each launched a single Type A. This deployment, given the eccentric operational name "Divine Turtle Operation Number One" by the IJN, occurred at a maximum distance of 13 miles from Pearl Harbor; several of the tenders moved closer.

The *USS Ward* sailed to the coordinates give by *Condor* but observed nothing. However, some time later, at 6:45 AM, a supply ship named the *SS Antares* spotted the midget again, and a PBY Catalina flying boat marked the spot with colored smoke. The *Ward* swooped in, and to their astonishment, Outerbridge and his crew saw a weird and unexpected craft amid the waves: "What he saw was a stubby black submarine, partly surfaced. It was smaller than any   U.S. submarine the *Ward's* crew had ever seen. Lieutenant Outerbridge was puzzled   by this strange craft, but his orders were clear: 'Depth bomb and sink any   submarines found in the defensive sea area.'" (Wills, 1991, 8).

The *USS Ward*

Some unknown mechanical fault clearly forced the midget sub's crew to surface, rendering it vulnerable to direct fire. The American gunners aimed true and a 4 inch shell punched through the submarine's thin skin at the base of the conning tower. The submarine, probably I-18tou, sank immediately.

Outerbridge, unable to tell if the midget sank or crash-dived to escape, ordered depth charges dropped. Divers located the sub in 2002, resting upright in the bottom muck, the skeletal remains of both crewmen, Furuno Shigema and Yokoyama Shigenori, inside. The Lieutenant sent a report to Pearl Harbor headquarters at 6:51 AM, though the HQ staff failed to raise the alarm: "We have attacked fired upon and dropped depth charges upon submarine operating in defense sea area." (Prenatt, 2014, 39).

The rest of the midget submarines suffered similar fates. American vessels spotted and depth-charged I-20tou in the shallow, calm waters of Keehi Lagoon, but a recovery crew later found the sub empty, its hatch opened from within, and containing only a pair of coveralls and a pair of shoes. The Americans found no trace of its crew, Hiro-o Akira and Katayama Yoshio.

The crew of I-22tou met a dramatic death, entering Pearl Harbor's North Channel and firing one of their torpedoes at *USS Curtiss,* a seaplane tender. *Curtiss'* crew fired a 5 inch shell into the midget, chopping the head neatly off Lieutenant Iwasa Naoji, standing in its conning tower. The destroyer *USS Monaghan,* which later saw action in the Aleutian Campaign, rammed

I-22tou and sank it, killing the other crew member, Sasaki Naokichi. The Americans returned Iwasa's body to Japan after the war, but filled the wreck with concrete with Sasaki's corpse still inside and used it as fill during pier construction.

Japanese Type A-class Midget Submarine I-22tou, Sunk inside Pearl Harbor, Hawaii

I-24tou ran aground ignominiously on a reef, though the crew managed to reverse off it once brought under fire by the destroyer *USS Helms.* However, leaking chlorine gas from the batteries forced the crew to surface and run the tiny vessel ashore at Waimanalo Beach. Struggling ashore through the surf, Inagaki Kiyoshi collapsed in the waves and died, probably from the effects of chlorine gas. Sakamaki Kazuo reached dry ground before collapsing unconscious, where an American patrol found him and took him prisoner. Sakamaki never returned to Japan due to the shame of his failure, living abroad for 30 years to atone for not having committed seppuku.

I-16tou, crewed by Yokoyama Masaharu and Kamita Sadamu, sank in the West Loch of Pearl Harbor, scuttled by its crew, who radioed news of their scuttling to the Japanese attack force. The fates of Yokoyama and Kamita remained unknown.

The recovered corpses and the single prisoner, Sakamaki, all carried escape and evasion maps of Oahu. The house of a Japanese-American resident, Dr. Yokichi Uyehara, bore the legend "Happy Mountain Retreat" on these maps. The day after the Pearl Harbor attack, a USN destroyer depth-charged and sank IJN submarine I-70, inexplicably lingering just offshore near Oahu's north coast, killing all hands.

The possibility remains that Yokoyama and Kamita from I-16tou and Hiro-o and Katayama from I-20tou survived, swam ashore, and used their escape and evasion maps to reach I-70, dying when it sank. Alternatively, they might have survived, contacted Dr. Uyehara or some other friendly Japanese-American, and permanently entered hiding, as even an American officer, Lieutenant Commander A.J. Stewart, later noted, "If they escaped from their boat after it had settled to the bottom […] they could   easily have melted into the local populace of Hawaii with its many Orientals. [...]   their determination to avoid capture might have caused them to seek aid from those   friendly to their cause […] Their devotion to Japanese ideology would likely have   caused them to reveal to no one [...] that they failed their mission. Therefore, it is a   remote possibility that [they] may be alive today." (Stewart, 1974, 63).

Regardless of the exact fate of the Type A midget submarine crews, the action at Pearl Harbor – and the Pacific war between the U.S. and the Empire of Japan – opened not with aircraft, but with submarine action. The Americans took a Japanese submariner as their first POW of the war. For the rest of the struggle, both sides employed submarines heavily, though with very different doctrines and highly divergent results.

World War II submarine warfare involved very different conditions from those experienced by submariners in the era of nuclear powered submarines. Conventional submarines, used by all navies in World War II, operated with diesel engines only usable while the submarine ran on the surface. Once submerged, the submarine could only operate using electric motors run by batteries.

Underwater, a submarine could choose to move quickly but exhaust its battery power in an hour or two, or conserve the batteries but move only very slowly. Heat built up rapidly inside a submerged "fish," soon topping 100 degrees Fahrenheit. The intense heat combined with battery fumes limited the time a submarine could remain under the surface. Eventually, temperatures rose to 125 degrees or higher. At this temperature, with breathing problems and battery fumes, men would begin to die after a time.

The record length for remaining submerged stood at approximately 38 hours, set by the USS Puffer and several Japanese I-boats. Some submarines probably remained submerged longer but their crews died and nobody survived to tell the tale.

The usual tactic consisted of prowling on the surface until the crew established visual or radar contact with an enemy ship. At that point, the submarine submerged to periscope depth and maneuvered to slip into firing range and achieve a good angle of attack, preferably launching torpedoes at right angles to the target's long axis. Periscopes could extend up to 12 feet above the water's surface like a metallic eyestalk, though the crew lowered them to 1 to 2 feet to reduce the chance of spotting as they moved closer to their quarry.

Following an attack, the submarine submerged to a considerably greater depth – thin-walled submarines could descend to 300 feet, while those with heavy hulls (such as American *Balao* and *Tench* classes) could reach 600 feet beneath the surface. There the submarine waited, powered down, and trying to avoid detection, until surface ships finished dropping depth charges in response to the attack. Then, the submarine used battery power to slip away to where it could surface, start its diesel engines, and depart the area rapidly.

If attacked on the surface, a submarine could "crash dive." This involved directing the bow planes downward, flooding the front ballast tanks, and switching off the diesel engines at precisely the moment the submarine plunged under the surface. The crew ran the electric motors at full power to shove the submarine downward quickly to the desired depth. World War II submarines possessed much superior crash diving capabilities than modern nuclear submarines, which can operate for extended periods underwater and therefore never risk the enemy catching them at the surface.

Japanese Submarines

In a certain sense, the midget submarine attack at Pearl Harbor on December 7th, 1941 summarized the entire history of the IJN submarine fleet during World War II. The Japanese developed technologically advanced submarines for their era, using unusual designs that startled their adversaries. However, instead of using these remarkable undersea vessels correctly, IJN planners frequently squandered them in inappropriate roles that minimized their unique strengths and often led to their futile destruction.

The Japanese originally intended their midget submarines – which evolved through Types A, B, C, and D during the war – for use in a large naval battle on the open ocean. The notable failure of the five midgets deployed at Pearl Harbor resulted at least partly from use of the tiny vessels for task ill-suited to their original purpose.

Type A Midget Submarine

Each midget sub carried two torpedoes, originally Type 97s and later Type 98s, each with a 772-lb explosive charge. Miniaturized versions of the superb Type 93 Long Lance torpedo, the Type 97/98s ran on a 38% oxygen fuel type (Campbell, 1985, 208), providing a range of 3,500 yards.

Captain Kishimoto Kaneharu developed the midget submarine for mass deployments during large fleet encounters between IJN and USN task forces. Released in vicious swarms, the midgets would move in swiftly and pepper American battleships and other large vessels with torpedoes, firing from all directions to make evasion impossible. Once each midget fired both torpedoes, it would retire to a predesignated rendezvous area, to be retrieved following the battle. Kishimoto did not design his midget submarines as suicide weapons, and therefore made the interior habitable for extended periods.

The midget submarines saw action a few more times following Pearl Harbor, though only once with any success. They never participated in a fleet battle as intended. Very late in the war, the Japanese modified some to use as suicide weapons by bolting a large magnetic mine to the nose, but none ever saw deployment in this role and the Americans found the uncompleted modifications after the cessation of hostilities.

The Imperial Japanese Navy took a distinctive approach to developing their submarine fleet. Where other navies produced a few versatile submarine types, which they then used as the basis for additional generations of vessels, the Japanese made many different submarine types and tried out a variety of experimental designs. Many IJN subs represented the largest submarines of the time, and served in unusual roles such as troop transports. Some even carried and launched smaller submarines or specialized seaplanes.

The main fleet submarine, the I-boat, came in a variety of configurations, including a command variant, a midget sub variant, a type with an internal watertight hangar for one scouting floatplane and a catapult for launching it, and a fourth type carrying extra torpedoes. The I-boat possessed an immense range, though onboard habitability remained low. The Japanese also used considerable resources making short-range RO-type coastal defense submarines, which remained highly ineffectual throughout the war.

World War I provided the Japanese in both an object lesson in the usefulness of submarines and material aid in starting their own program. The Japanese government focused on the use of seapower to project their influence from the victories of the Russo-Japanese War of 1905 onward. Imperial planners and naval commanders took careful note of the damage done to shipping by the German U-boats of World War I.

Following Germany's surrender in 1918, the Japanese received 7 U-boats as their share of war reparations. They also hired dozens of German naval engineers and scientists to disassemble the U-boats and teach Japanese experts every detail of submarine design, materials science, and construction then known. In just one decade, the Japanese scientists learned enough to not only start a homegrown submarine industry without any further aid from foreigners, but also to make fresh and unique technological advances.

Rear Admiral Nobumasa Suetsugu developed the conceptual and doctrinal framework that shaped Japanese submarine design choices. Nobumasa conceived of submarines in an aggressive role, able to project Japanese power at locations remote from the shores of the home islands. Accordingly, the subs produced needed immense range to reach their operational area with potentially minimal support, plus great toughness and seaworthiness to stand up to lengthy tours of duty in the rigorous Pacific environment.

Rear Admiral Nobumasa Suetsugu

The Japanese therefore focused on big submarines, able to carry large amounts of fuel and supplies and large enough to endure hazardous weather and other risks. Powerful engines made these submarines capable of moving at high speeds for extended periods, quickly reaching and, hopefully, dominating waters far from their home port in the gigantic expanses of the Pacific Ocean.

Japan built submarines for one eventuality above all others: fighting the United States. The Imperial government thoughts war with America, fought with fleets, absolutely unavoidable from the 1920s onward. The strategic plan for this conflict involved letting the American fleet advance into the Western Pacific, where the main fleet of surface ships would engage and destroy it.

However, along the way, fast, long-range, powerful submarines would stalk and hunt the American ships, pouncing on the USN vessels in repeated ambushes and destroying many of the most powerful before they reached the final battleground. The submarines would harry the American fleets like predators, greatly weakening the loathed foreigners' vessel strength prior to the decisive clash and weighting the outcome in Japan's favor. The idea of attacking supply lines and sinking oilers, cargo ships, and the like did not enter into Japanese strategic thinking.

The Japanese chiefly used the Type 89, Type 93, and Type 95 torpedoes. These torpedoes possessed an extremely long range of up to 43,700 yards, and carried a 1,080 lb warhead. Running on oxygen, these torpedoes left almost no wake on the sea surface, making them difficult to detect and elude. They proved devastatingly effective from the start of the war, and the Japanese used variants of them throughout.

Type 93 Torpedo

Part of the reason for the Type 93 "Long Lance" torpedo's effectiveness resulted from extensive testing against actual unmanned ships used as targets. The Imperial Japanese Navy's advantage over the navies of other nations in this regard lay in their effectively open-ended expense account.

Where different countries concerned themselves with spending too much taxpayer money, the Japanese military viewed that the rest of society existed to support them. The IJN bought as many ships as needed, and destroyed them, to work out the problems and hone the features of the Type 93 torpedo.

American Submarines

Towards the start of the war, the U.S. deployed mostly S-class submarines, a nearly obsolete type rapidly replaced by more advanced models. Soon, the *Gato*-class joined the lineup. This 311-foot vessel featured 6 fore and 4 aft torpedo tubes, plus a 3-inch deck gun, and 20mm and 40mm anti-aircraft cannons. The *Gato* could dive safely to a depth of 300 feet. In 1943, the USN introduced the *Balao*-class, an improved *Gato* with a 5-inch deck gun and a nominal test depth of 400 feet, though submariners soon proved it could descend safely to 600 feet due to its robust hull.

American submarines displayed generally high quality and good design, but used the extremely problematic Type XIV torpedo. This 21-inch torpedo suffered from several problems, including a faulty triggering mechanism that rendered most torpedoes duds and a tendency to run too deep. The Board of Ordnance eventually corrected these faults, after which the Type XIV functioned quite well, though with a shorter range than the Type 93.

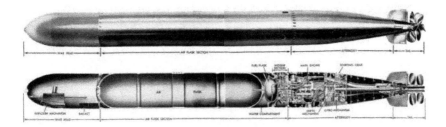

The Mark XIV Torpedo

U.S. submarine design emphasized habitability in a way the Japanese did not. A powerful air conditioning system provided the centerpiece of this design decision. The interior still grew uncomfortably hot when not running at the surface with the hatches open, but the air conditioning served two valuable functions.

It lessened crew fatigue, enabling faster responses and greater crew effectiveness. It also reduced the massive condensation caused by overheating, which, on a submarine lacking air conditioning, could actually grow intense enough to cause electrical shorts in vital equipment. The dehumidifying effects of the air conditioning made American submarines from the *Gato*-class onward very mechanically reliable.

Gato and *Balao* class submarines also included washing machines, small lockers for personal belongings, and even cramped showers for the crew, in addition to refrigerated food storage. Though derided as luxuries by German U-boat veterans, these features maintained crew morale and, to some extent, physical condition during the extremely long patrols through tropical seas characteristic of U.S. Pacific submarine operations.

USS Gato

Submarines from Pearl Harbor to Operation Cactus

The United States already maintained a submarine presence in East Asian waters prior to the outbreak of World War II, with dozens of submarines stationed at Manila in the Philippines. The Japanese began bombing Manila on December 10th, 1941, just three days after the Pearl Harbor strike. The American submarines abandoned the base to avoid destruction, while the *USS Sealion*, undergoing repairs at Cavite Naval Yard in Cavite City, Philippines suffered destruction due to Japanese bombs.

Immediately before the attack, Captain Stuart "Sunshine" Murray sent 18 submarines out on fleet patrol. His speech to the submarines' commanders underlined the need to conserve the vessels rather than take needless or heroic risks: "Listen, dammit [...] Don't try to go out there and win the Congressional Medal of Honor in one day. The submarines are all we have left. Your crews are more valuable than anything else. Bring them back." (Blair, 2001, 131).

The strike on Cavite destroyed much of the Americans' Western Pacific torpedo stockpile, also, in addition to killing over 500 men and damaging the submarine *USS Seadragon*. Bombing attacks on Manila continued through the new year, with much indiscriminate damage inflicted on the city.

The American submarines on patrol split up, and soon encountered heavy Japanese ship traffic as the IJN reinforced the imperial push southwards. Some of the U.S. subs ventured as far north as Vietnam, where the Japanese maintained several large, important naval bases at the time. Weather conditions kept the submarines well below the surface except when rising to periscope depth prior to an attack.

The American submarines attacked many transports, destroyers, and in one case a carrier. However, they achieved no kills. A few torpedoes detonated prematurely, in several cases coming close to damaging the submarine launching them. In all other cases, the torpedoes failed to detonate at all. The skippers began to suspect – correctly – that the Mark VI magnetic exploder bore responsibility. These faulty devices made American torpedoes almost useless during the opening days of the war.

American submarines scored occasional successes despite the problems with the Mark VI, which functioned in certain conditions and areas unpredictably. By the end of January 1942, however, dozens of subs had sunk just 9 Japanese ships, all of them poorly armed supply ships and freighters, and many of them quite small. At the start of February, 26 submarines remained, based temporarily at Surabaya until the Japanese tide overwhelmed that location also.

One of the biggest early-war USN submarine successes occurred on February 8th, 1942, when S-37 commanded by James Dempsey encountered the huge Makassar City invasion force, a large convoy of Japanese transports steaming through the darkness with a very strong destroyer escort. Dempsey and his crew tried to maneuver into position to attack the transports, but when this proved impossible, "he decided to attempt to bump off some of the "tin cans," as destroyers are   irreverently known [...] Dempsey launched a series of torpedoes at the convoy and watched in awe as the third destroyer in line, the 1,900 ton Natushio, went up in an orange ball of flame." (Whitlock, 2007, 37).

Dempsey's vessel survived the inevitable barrage of depth charges unleashed by the other ships guarding the convoy. The daring captain kept his nearly obsolete submarine in action for the next 17 days against the Makassar City force, but the unreliable torpedoes in the S-37's tubes foiled every other attempt to harm a Japanese ship.

In February 1942, the Americans also made use of a submarine for one of the periodic clandestine missions the design of these secretive craft suited them to. The Philippine government sent their treasury to the United States for safekeeping aboard the USS Trout, Michael Fenno commanding.

The Trout took on 6.5 tons of gold and 630 sacks of silver coins at Corregidor, The vessel then successfully eluded the Japanese and reached Pearl Harbor with its valuable cargo. The U.S. government stored the gold and silver at Fort Knox for the duration of the war, then returned the full amount to the Philippine government following the struggle.

As the Japanese advance continued relentlessly south through the Western Pacific islands, the American submarines fell back to bases first in Java, then in Australia itself. During this period, the Japanese managed to destroy five more American submarines, mostly through the use of depth charges, and captured the crew of the *USS Perch* on March 3rd, interning the prisoners at a characteristically hellish POW camp.

The Americans and Australians decided on using Fremantle as the main western Pacific base for Allied submarines throughout the war, starting in March, 1942. Ultimately, 127 USN subs used the Fremantle base, along with 31 British Royal Navy and 10 Dutch submarines. The Allies selected Fremantle in Western Australia due to the fact it lay outside the range of Japanese land-based bombers in the islands.

The first 10 American submarines arrived on March 10th, by which time a trio of Dutch K-class subs also used the harbor. The American crews soon discovered a strong streak of hospitality in their Australian hosts, as well as an abundant supply of beef, pastimes such as kangaroo hunting and horseback riding, and attractive young women (many of whom eventually married visiting "Yanks" despite military regulations designed to discourage the practice).

Fremantle provided a far more important setting for the future of American submarine warfare than a source of entertainment and matrimony for USN submariners. The new commanders of the base used the waters nearby for extensive testing of American torpedoes, which finally and objectively proved the need for new, better designs. This occurred thanks to the initiative of the 1942 American base commander, Charles Lockwood, who "ordered a test of the torpedoes. On June 20, 1942, *USS Skipjack* fired its last three   torpedoes at five hundred feet of fishnet stretched across Frenchman's Bay [...] The   tests confirmed what many submarine skippers had been claiming for months: the   torpedoes ran deeper than set and often undershot their intended target." (Sturma, 2015, 38).

Despite the critical role of Australia in keeping far-flung American operations in the Pacific supplied, the Japanese made only a brief submarine incursion into Australian waters, between March and August, 1942.

IJN fleet doctrine largely discounted the role of submarines as independent commerce raiders, so such raiding, though it occurred, transpired at a much lower level than the Americans, Germans, or indeed any other fleet deploying submarines in World War II. The submarines also used their deck guns to ineffectively shell several Australian port cities, producing widespread alarm but contributing nothing of tactical or strategic value to the IJN war effort.

Divine Turtle Operation Number Two

Undeterred by the failure of midget submarines on the offensive in Pearl Harbor, the Japanese made a second attempt to use these small, stealthy craft to attack ships at anchor early in 1942. In April to May, the southern hemisphere autumn, three IJN I-boats, I-22, I-24, and I-27, set out from Truk with the improved Type A Kai 1 and E14Y floatplanes aboard. They sailed for Sydney Harbor, hoping to find berthed Australian warships. The plan called for a fourth submarine, I-28, to join them, but the American sub *USS Tautog* caught I-28 on the surface and destroyed it with three torpedoes, killing its 88-man crew.

The IJN showed a commendable lack of superstition by naming the plan Divine Turtle Operation Number Two, a clear followup on the Pearl Harbor fiasco. Repeated reconnaissance flights by E14Y floatplanes revealed ships in the harbor. Captain Izu Juichi on I-29, prowling near Sydney, misidentified an American ship entering the harbor as the battleship *HMS Warspite*, a major feather in the submariners' caps if the midgets sank it.

HMS Warspite

The Japanese submarines arrived off Sydney on May 31st, 1942, a cold day of strong south winds and blustering, unpleasant rain squalls under a low cloud deck. The Australian, American, and British military personnel crowding the city showed little alertness, staying indoors in taverns, brothels, and casinos to avoid the wet, chilly weather.

Accordingly, the Japanese waited for nightfall and released three midgets at a distance of 6 miles from the harbor entrance. Knowing the results of the first Divine Turtle Operation, the submariners exhibited a bleak mood, echoed by the I-boat crews. Ito Susumo, a reconnaissance pilot, recalled the feelings of the men that night: "It was heart-rending for those of us who sent them off […] We knew it was for the   sake of our country, but it would cost the lives of six young men. It was so painful   to see them go to an almost certain death. We wished they would somehow manage   to come back alive." (Grose, 2007, 95).

Sydney Harbor's defenses included an extensive, but not fully finished, boom net for blocking submarines, its lower edge unusually anchored to the sea floor, and metal-detecting "detector loops" laid on the seabed to monitor all incoming and outgoing traffic.

The Australians detected the first midget sub when it ran afoul of the unfinished boom net at around 8 PM. A night watchman named Jimmy Cargill, charged with guarding the boom construction materials from theft, spotted the midget while out checking on the construction cranes in a 14 foot skiff. Cargill rowed close in to the small submarine, noting its paired external torpedo tubes, but thought it a floating mine.

Cargill rowed to one of the harbor patrol boats, the *HMAS Yarroma*, and asked its skipper, Harold Eyers, to investigate. Initially reluctant, Eyers eventually sent a man with Cargill to examine the object. By this time, the midget sub ran its engines furiously, trying to break free of the net, and the two men immediately identified it as a submarine. The midget sub apparently struck the base of a harbor light underwater, reversed, and backed straight into the adjacent net.

HMAS Yarroma

After lengthy and frequently failed attempts at communication, Eyers sent another patrol boat, *HMAS Lolita* under Harold Anderson, to deal with the midget. Anderson later reported what he saw: "Inspected object by flashing Aldis Lamp on it, which proved to be a submarine. [...]   She was inside the net, her bow being approximately two feet above water, periscope showing about a foot, and stern entirely submerged. She appeared to be struggling to extricate herself. I realized at once the necessity for immediate action and gave the order to stand by depth charges." (Grose, 2007, 115).

Lolita dropped two depth charges, but both failed to detonate due to being set to explode at 100 feet but hit bottom at 81 feet. However, as the patrol boat approached a third time, the midget sub exploded as its commander, Lieutenant Chuman Kenshi, set off its scuttling charge. The explosion almost capsized the *Lolita*.

The sound of the blast finally put Sydney on the alert. The second midget slipped into the harbor in the wake of a passenger ferry, and the third entered very late, picked out almost immediately by the searchlight beam from the patrol boat *Lauriana*. *HMAS Yandra* under James Taplin rammed the third midget but failed to sink it, as did depth charges the *Yandra* dropped.

The men on the American cruiser *USS Chicago* spotted the midget's conning tower and fired wildly at it with anti-aircraft guns, 5 inch guns, and the .45 pistol of an officer on the deck, but failed to score a hit despite the torrent of fire they loosed into the night.

The midget, eluding both fire and pursuit, fired two torpedoes from abaft the *USS Chicago*, narrowly missing it to the right and left. In a turn of events that would be comedic if not for the deaths inflicted on that night, Captain Howard Bode of the *Chicago*, already utterly hated by his officers and men, busily harangued them for firing at nonexistent submarines at precisely the moment one of the torpedoes struck a seawall just past his vessel and exploded, as an officer, George Kitteridge, reported: "It was obviously a torpedo wake and everybody said: look at that, look at that.   Bode looked over and said: Hmp! It's just a motor launch going by. Just when he   said that he faced us again. His back was towards the bow, and boom!." (Grose, 2007, 142).

The explosion annihilated the former civilian ferry *Kuttabul*, tied up alongside the seawall, and killed 21 of the 31 men on board. The second torpedo failed to arm and did not detonate. The firing now picked up intensely again, but came nowhere near the midgets.

Having fired both torpedoes, the third Type A now slipped out of the harbor at 2 AM. The *USS Chicago* and several other large ships followed, looking to escape any other lurking midgets. By a supreme tactical oversight, the Japanese commander failed to have even a single I-boat on ambush station, ready to sink escaping ships.

As the *Chicago* left the harbor, the second midget passed close by it at the surface, too close to be fired upon. Captain Bode goggled at the small sub as it slid past into the harbor in search of quarry, his denials finally silenced. A game of cat and mouse then followed for most of the night, as the second sub's torpedoes both failed to fire. A depth charge from the patrol boat *Sea Mist* finally blew it in half, and the captain shot his crewman in the back of the head before committing suicide himself.

The third Type A escaped the harbor but failed to rendezvous with the waiting I-boats. The crew clearly attempted to survive, conserving battery power, firing their torpedoes at an angle to make a quick getaway, and slipping out of the harbor. However, divers found the wreck of the sub 9.7 miles away to the north in 2006, near Newport Reef. The fate of the crew remains unknown, with suicide the most likely possibility.

Japanese and American Campaigns

In early June, 1942, a decisive clash occurred between the fleets of Admirals Yamamoto Isoroku of the IJN and Chester Nimitz of the USN at Midway. One American submarine, the *USS Nautilus,* achieved a single utterly ineffective torpedo hit on a Japanese carrier during the struggle and barely escaped the frenzied deployment of depth charges ensuing. Aircraft decided the outcome of the encounter, which sent Japan's finest carriers to the bottom and set the stage for an American counteroffensive.

Chester Nimitz

Operation Cactus, the first USN offensive of the Pacific Theater, began in August 1942. However, the submarines, still defanged by their low-quality torpedoes, contributed very little to maritime warfare during the rest of 1942.

The American Bureau of Ordnance repeatedly refused to accept the results of Lockwood's Fremantle torpedo tests, even when subsequent tests duplicated the results. Lockwood appealed directly to Admiral Ernest King, who used his much greater military and political leverage to compel the Bureau of Ordnance to carry out thorough tests.

This revealed the massive shortcomings of the Mark XIV torpedo, including its tendency to run far deeper than set and the near uselessness of the magnetic "pistol" detonating the warhead. Furthermore, the tests revealed weak firing pins that bent rather than exploding the warhead, causing the frequently observed problem of torpedoes striking enemy hulls and not triggering.

While the Bureau of Ordnance worked frantically on sturdier firing pins and other improvements, its headquarters issued an advisory memo suggesting submariners fire their torpedoes to strike at a glancing angle as a stopgap measure, rather than at right angles to the enemy hull. Such an angled strike proved much less likely to bend the firing pins. However, it required much more luck and better conditions to reliably make a difficult angled shot, particularly against a moving target.

On the Japanese side, the I-boats continued their history of tactical excellence and strategic futility through the rest of 1942. The Japanese stationed 9 I-boats off specific river and harbor mouths along the West Coast of the U.S., including Washington, Oregon, and California. With their immense operational range and excellent seaworthiness, the I-boats had no problem in reaching these locations or remaining on station there.

With their emphasis on attacking the biggest military ships and to avoid most contacts with merchant shipping to avoid drawing attention to themselves, the West Coast I-boats sank just 5 freighters and oilers, inflicting a loss of slightly under 31,000 tons of shipping. One submarine, *I-27*, shelled an oil derrick at one point, inflicting little damage but leading to Radio Tokyo to bombastically declare that "sensible Americans know the submarine shelling of the Pacific coast was a   warning to the nation that the Paradise created by George Washington is on the verge of destruction. […] as the Imperial Navy now controls all the Pacific and   Indian Oceans, the day is imminent when these will be called the New Sea of   Japan." (Boyd, 1995, 61).

The Japanese sent submarines to Wake Island, Rabaul, and the Bismarck Islands during their occupation of these locations, where the undersea vessels contributed absolutely nothing to the beach assaults. Instead, they lurked offshore, colliding with one another and occasionally fatally running aground on coral reefs.

Sometimes, IJN submarines provided an effective scouting force, as at the invasion of Malaya. There, Submarine Squadron 4 located *HMS Prince of Wales* and *Repulse*. Though torpedo attacks failed notably, Lieutenant Commander Kitamura Soshichi aboard *I-58* maintained contact and radioed regular position updates. This enabled Japanese torpedo bombers to zero in on the luckless British capital ships and sink them on December 10th.

Similarly, on December 26th and the following days, 25 I-boats supported the invasion of the Dutch East Indies and sank 40 Dutch cargo ships in a brief span of time. This action helped to starve the defenders of supplies and materiel and contributed directly to the success of Japanese land forces.

1943

A decisive shift occurred in Pacific submarine warfare during 1943. Swarms of new American submarines arrived from shipyards on the east and west coasts, and even inland facilities, such as the Manitowoc Shipbuilding Company, located in the eponymous city and on the river of the same name in Wisconsin, which produced 28 submarines during the war.

Additionally, gifted submarine skippers whose grasp of "silent service" tactics gave them a lethal edge in their hunter-killer missions emerged among the U.S. Navy personnel. As the year continued, improved torpedoes put in an appearance, causing Japanese shipping losses to skyrocket – though still at a rate below that achieved in 1944 and 1945.

Spearheading the newly aggressive chapter in American submarine warfare stood a single man, Dudley "Mush" Morton, the skipper of the *USS Wahoo*. The nickname derived from Morton's huge, prominent jaw which resembled that of the character "Mushmouth" in the comic strip "Moon Mullins." Morton played up the physical feature as something of a trademark, frequently demonstrating his ability to stuff four golf balls into his mouth simultaneously.

USS Wahoo

"Mush" Morton declared the *Wahoo* expendable, existing for the purpose of sinking Japanese ships of any kind wherever encountered, and allowed any man uncomfortable with this arrangement to transfer off. Morton's skill as skipper and his expansive personality both endeared him to the all-volunteer, gung-ho crew he thus assembled: "He was always roaming around the narrow quarters, [...] his wide-set eyes missing nothing. He was built like a bear, and as playful as cub. His authority was built-in and never depended on sudden stiffening of tone or attitude. [...] The men were not merely ready to follow him, they were eager to." (Wheeler, 1998, 64).

Another man soon to prove a popular, and extremely effective, submarine skipper served as his executive officer, Lieutenant Richard O'Kane. Tightly wound, with intense eyes and compressed lips, O'Kane talked incessantly and ferociously, but unlike many men exhibiting constant verbal aggression, the Lieutenant soon proved himself a dangerous opponent to the Japanese and a surprisingly popular commander in turn.

"Mush" Morton's first raid involved infiltration of the heavily defended Weak Harbor, where the *Wahoo* first attacked a Japanese destroyer. The submarine fired three torpedoes, all apparent duds, and dove to avoid the inevitable retribution. A gigantic explosion smashed light bulbs inside, which the men interpreted as a depth charge letting loose. However, no others followed, and when a stunned crewman suggested that the blast might have been the destroyer exploding, "Mush" Morton, roaring with laughter, ordered the sub to periscope depth. The men saw the destroyer sinking and turned towards other game.

The *Wahoo* sank a transport, the *Buyo Maru,* and a freighter in Wewak Harbor also. The Japanese soldiers escaping the transport made the error of firing at the *Wahoo*, and "Mush" Morton opened fire on them with the sub's deck guns for 15 minutes before sailing away, though the majority survived. *Wahoo*'s crew tied a broom onto the mast when entering Pearl Harbor, emblematic of a "clean sweep," and the submarine earned the sobriquet "the one-boat wolf-pack."

Morton's actions in firing on the transport survivors verged on a war crime, if they did not actually constitute one, similar to the common Japanese practice of machine-gunning survivors which drew opprobrium from all quarters. Though not censured at the time, Morton immediately became a controversial figure, and the board reviewing his eligibility for a Medal of Honor declined to grant it for unspecified reasons, though probably as a tacit condemnation of Morton's hate-fueled attack on the men in the water.

Richard O'Kane soon commanded his own boat, the *USS Tang,* which racked up an impressive score of ship kills before its eventual sinking by one of its own torpedoes and the capture and torture of some of the crew at a Japanese facility known as the "Torture Farm."

1943 also witnessed the introduction of the *Balao*-class submarine to the USN. The existing *Gato*-class already exhibited great technological and operational excellence, with the exception of the Mark XIV torpedo's defects. The *Balao*-class represented an even more formidable undersea hunter-killer, with thicker hull plates made of high yield strength steel, enabling deeper dives (up to 600 feet) and thus better evasion of depth charges. O'Kane's lethal *USS Tang* was a *Balao*-class, and the new submarines proved destined to sweep Japanese shipping from the seas.

The Bureau of Ordnance finally improved the Mark XIV to the limits of its rather imperfect design by September 1943. A new triggering device ensured the torpedo now usually detonated when it hit the target, rather than proving a dud 70% or more of the time. Now functional, and fitted to high-quality submarines with one of the world's earliest targeting computers aboard, the Mark XIV began exacting a deadly toll.

In the meantime, however, many commanders continued to disbelieve submarine skippers' reports that their torpedoes ran erratically or proved duds when they struck home.

Instead, they chalked the failures up to poor marksmanship or skillful Japanese maneuvering. On several occasions, submarine skippers and their port-bound commanders, who never participated personally in the patrols, nearly came to physical blows during arguments about the torpedoes, as Lawson P. "Red" Ramage reported after an altercation with Admiral Ralph Christie: "When we got outside Christie's office, McLean said, 'You're goddamned lucky to be   going to sea.'. I said, 'It's the other way around, Tex. With these torpedoes you're giving us, I'll be goddamned lucky to get back. If you think I'm so lucky, how about   packing your bag and corning along with me?' That cooled him." (Blair, 2001, 391).

American submarines continued to operate out of Fremantle, now under the command of Ralph Christie following Charles Lockwood's promotion to Admiral and appointment to overall command of the entire USN submarine service. During the first part of 1943, these submarines carried out 22 patrols, resulting in 23 Japanese vessels confirmed sunk and the loss of two American subs.

The Mark XVIII electric wakeless torpedo, under development for some time, first saw limited deployment in mid to late 1943, despite delays caused by inter-office rivalries and technical problems. The torpedo proved frequently effective, and represented about 30% of the total number of torpedoes fired in the Pacific theater. Nevertheless, a rare but persistent fault sometimes caused the Mark XVIII to run in a complete circle and return to sink the submarine that launched it.

On October 11th, 1943, Dudley "Mush" Morton's brief but successful career came to an abrupt end, as did that of the *Wahoo* and its crew. O'Kane, though not yet given his own command, did not participate in the *Wahoo's* terminal patrol, having been transferred off in one of the many reshufflings of personnel common in the wartime submarine service.

Morton's cheerful brand of aggression contributed to his death, and under his command, the *USS Wahoo* entered the Sea of Japan, the first U.S. submarine to do so since the commencement of hostilities. The vessel torpedoed the steamer *Konron Maru* in Tsushima Strait, killing over 500 of the 616 Japanese on board. *Time* magazine trumpeted, "The Tsushima Straits are Japan's historic doors to the Asiatic mainland [...]   Presumably the submarine knocking on the door last week was American. It had achieved one of World War II's most daring submarine penetrations of enemy   waters, a feat ranking with German Günther Prien's entry at Scapa Flow, the Jap   invasion of Pearl Harbor, the U.S. raid in Tokyo Bay." (Scott, 2013, 115).

However, "Mush" Morton stuck his neck out too far on this occasion, and the margin for error in the "silent service" remained paper-thin. On October 11th, 1943, a Japanese aircraft dropped three depth charges on a suspected submarine at *Wahoo's* approximate location. Patrol boats sent to the area by the IJN reported an oil slick and large air bubbles, indicating a probable sinking, and, the next day, found part of an American submarine propeller washed up on a nearby shore. The Americans never heard from the submarine or its crew again.

At the same time, the submarine fleet at Pearl Harbor underwent a massive expansion as new subs built in Manitowoc, Wisconsin, Mare Island, California, Portsmouth, and other locations began arriving in considerable numbers. Mostly *Gato*-class submarines at this point in the war, these "fish" still proved dangerous to the Japanese, particularly once the improved Mark XIV torpedoes began arriving in September.

Japanese shipping losses rose steeply in 1943 as these new submarines began crisscrossing the deep blue, sun-shot, storm-lashed Pacific waters. Soon, the Americans sank more than 100,000 tons of shipping per month. However, a famous indiscretion on the part of an American politician provided the Japanese with at least some revenge for the destruction.

Kentucky Congressman Andrew Jackson May spoke to the press in June 1943 and declared that many American submarines survived because the Japanese set their depth bomb fuses to explode at too shallow a depth. On top of this gaffe, dozens of papers, including those of Honolulu, Hawaii (a city definitely riddled with Japanese spies during World War II), gleefully and irresponsibly published this as headline news. The Japanese soon increased the depth on their depth bomb fuzes and American submarine losses rose. Vice Admiral Charles Lockwood responded bitterly to this huge security breach:

Lockwood wrote Admiral Edwards in acid words, "1 hear Congressman May said the Jap depth charges are not set deep enough. He would be pleased to know the   Japs set 'em deeper now." And after the war, Lockwood wrote, "I consider that   indiscretion cost us ten submarines and 800 officers and men" (Blair, 2001, 424).

May went on to involve himself in further scandals, and served 9 months in Federal prison for taking bribes from a munitions manufacturer, Murray Garsson, who supplied 4.2-inch mortar shells that exploded in the barrel due to poor design, killing a total of 35 American soldiers.

Postwar records revealed the American submarine force in the Pacific collectively sank approximately 335 Japanese ships in 1943, totaling around 1.5 million tons, at a cost of 15 submarines lost. Though the number of Japanese tankers rose due to a frantic building program, other shipping suffered a net decline of approximately one-sixth, seriously cutting into the import of bulk commodities and thus slowing the manufacture of new materiel for the war.

As the Americans began putting the Japanese on the defensive, the IJN started wasting its remaining I-boats' efforts even more on ill-conceived missions. While commendable, the desire to rescue cut-off garrisons on remote islands using I-boats tied up these large, dangerous craft in "taxi missions" and led to very high losses of valuable submarines and experienced crews in some cases.

Nevertheless, those submarines actually used in an aggressive role scored some notable successes, indicating how much damage the IJN might have inflicted with well-directed and offensive-oriented submarine strategy. On September 13th, 1942, Commander Kinashi Takaichi attacked a small U.S. carrier force south of San Cristobal Island. His submarine, *I-19*, fired six Type 95 torpedoes, inflicting fatal damage on the destroyer *USS O'Brien* and scoring three hits on *USS Wasp*, CV-7, sinking the vessel and killing 193 of its 2,167 crew.

USS Wasp

During this period, Japan also began the program of sending submarines around the world into the Atlantic to make contact with Nazi Germany and exchange war materials. Frequently ill-fated, these expeditions raised Allied fears of Axis development of nuclear weapons via scientific exchanges between the Japanese and Third Reich.

Admiral Ugaki Matome, who later committed suicide by *kamikaze* attack after Japan's surrender, described the fate of one of these submarines, destroyed by a mine after nearly completing its epic voyage: "The most regrettable incident was the sinking of the submarine *I-30*. After the Indian Ocean operation she was sent to Europe and, after sailing around South Africa, arrived safely at a German submarine base in France [...] A big welcome given to her was made public in radio, photos, and announcements by Imperial headquarters. On her way back, she reached Singapore [...] But she struck a mine at the end of the swept channel south of the commercial port and sank." (Boyd, 1995, 92).

Though all but 12 of the crew escaped, the Japanese lost the weapons and materials aboard. The Japanese did receive acoustic mines from Germany, however, which *I-6* laid off Brisbane to test them on Allied shipping. Other submarines rescued soldiers and sailors from Japanese transports sunk by American subs or air attacks.

Following the defeat of their ill-conceived invasion of the Aleutian Islands off Alaska, the Japanese also deployed a number of I-boats there in an effort to rescue the garrison of Kiska Island before the Americans attacked it. While the submarines managed to rescue a few hundred soldiers, the Americans sank three, including one laden with military evacuees.

Admiral Kiwase Shiro called off the operation, instead using destroyers to rescue nearly 3,000 Japanese soldiers from the island at the moment when the American blockading force sailed away to engage in the "Battle of the Pips," firing at radar images probably caused by dense flocks of dusky shearwaters feeding on schooling pollock.

The Japanese carried out limited commerce raiding in the Indian Ocean in 1943, and also used I-boats to put Indian revolutionaries such as Subhas Chandra Bose ashore to cause trouble for the British. Bose's insertion into British territory after years of exile in Nazi Germany, involving his transfer from a U-boat to an I-boat in the middle of the Indian Ocean, represents the stuff of adventure novels brought to life. However, these operations remained so circumscribed by the Japanese fixation with using their submarines during a decisive "battleship encounter" with the U.S. fleet that they did no more than highlight the wasted potential of the IJN submarine force in World War II.

The Fate of Prisoners

As with land forces, the Japanese Navy showed an alarming eagerness to commit atrocities against captured enemy sailors and hapless civilians alike. IJN officers commonly rewarded good performance aboard submarines with "hunting licenses" permitting the men to rape any local civilian women they fancied. Japanese prison guards also vented their cruelty on captured submariners on numerous occasions.

Though the Americans captured very few Japanese sailors, those rare prisoners typically received contrastingly kind treatment from their U.S. captors. The submariners of the *USS Tang* once rescued a man by name of Mishuitunni Ka from the sea, nicknaming him Firecracker since they took him prisoner on Independence Day 1944. As later recalled, "he was treated more like a guest of honor: One midnight, while passing through the   galley, [Captain Richard] O'Kane had found a cook hard at work. 'Oh, I'm just   trying to get the texture of Firecracker's rice the way he's used to it, Captain,' the cook had commented. 'We've been cooking it too hard.'" (Kershaw, 2008, 142).

The treatment O'Kane and his surviving crew suffered after the accidental sinking of *USS*

Tang by one of its own Mark XVIII torpedoes contrasted sharply with this sentimentality. After the six men survived a difficult ascent of 180 feet from the sunken *Balao*-class submarine (two more died almost immediately from the effects of decompression after reaching the surface), the Japanese caught them and subjected them to beatings, torture through confinement in a tiny metal shed in the sun, waterboarding, starvation, exposure to swarms of mosquitoes, and other methods.

While O'Kane and his men suffered terribly, they survived the war, as many others did not. The Japanese guards at many facilities proved all too willing to take out frustrations of defeat by murdering prisoners, often in the most agonizing and barbaric ways possible. The four survivors of the submarine *USS Rubalo,* including its skipper Captain M.M. Kimmel, perished in reprisal for an air raid: "[W]hen some Allied aircraft attacked Palawan, the Japanese became enraged, 'went   into a frenzy, pushed Kimmel and some other POWs in a ditch, then poured gasoline into the ditch and set it on fire.'" (Blair, 2001, 688).

The Imperial Japanese Navy also made a custom of machine gunning survivors and lifeboats after a sinking. Though "Mush" Morton committed a similar act in 1943, his action remained controversial, cost him a medal, and shocked many of his crew. The Japanese, however, performed such acts frequently and casually, and often with cruel flourishes seemingly designed purely for the sake of malice.

As just one example, on March 26th, 1944, *I-8* sank the Dutch merchant ship *Tjisalak,* and the Japanese captain, Ariizumi Tatsunosuke ordered all of the inflatable life rafts of sunken vessel riddled with bullets. The Japanese then ceased fire, allowing the survivors to scramble up onto the submarine itself, the only available refuge. Once every man was aboard, the Japanese attacked them with pistols, bayonets, swords, clubs, hammers, and large wrenches, hacking and beating 100 of the 105 trapped men to death and then submerging to drown any wounded survivors of the butchery.

Ariizumi Tatsunosuke

Five of the injured men survived, however, by swimming to a damaged but still floating life raft, including the Dutchmen Frits de Jong, Jan Dekker, and Cees Spuybroek, the English wireless operator James Blears, and a Laskar sailor identified only as Dhange. A passing Liberty Ship rescued the men, while Ariizumi went on to commit a number of similar war crimes.

Ariizumi's actions, though involving a unique *modus operandi* with the use of hammers and wrenches as the weapons of massacre, fell within the typical range of IJN behavior. Japanese submariners displayed almost sublime courage on a number of occasions, yet also repeatedly and willingly engaged acts of almost incredible slaughter, rapine, and torture.

1944-1945

Throughout 1944 and into 1945, the U.S. Navy and Marines steadily crushed the forces of the Japanese Empire, like an incoming steel tsunami. From the two surviving carriers after Pearl Harbor, the ocean soon teemed with over 100 American aircraft carriers, while most of Japan's lay at the bottom of the sea.

The skies teemed with F4F Wildcats, F6F Hellcats, P-38 Lightnings, and other tough, powerful fighters flown by increasingly skilled U.S. airmen. The island-hopping campaign rolled ever closer to the Japanese homeland, underlining the helplessness of the brave but outnumbered and outfought men of the IJN and IJA to stop an inevitable American victory.

Under the sea, America's submarines achieved full maturity as a deadly striking force from the start of 1944 until the end of the war. With improved torpedoes rounding out the superb capabilities of the USN's submarines, these vessels exacted an unprecedented toll from the Japanese despite representing only a tiny sliver of the naval might brought to bear by the United States.

Operating alone or in small, highly aggressive wolf-packs, the *Gato*-class submarines, now augmented by *Balao*-class types and a handful of *Tench*-class boats, sent hundreds of Japanese freighters and tankers to the bottom. This deprived Japan of raw materials such as iron and rubber, reduced the food supply, and cut down sharply on the amount of oil available to run Japan's ships, vehicles, and factories. The famous Richard O'Kane described a scene repeated over a thousand times during the Pacific war:

A whack, a flash, and a tremendous rumble came from the freighter's stern. Then from amidships, and her whole side seemed ripped out. The countdown was resumed only to be smothered in two more explosions. The second ship's stern was a mass of flames, and her superstructure aft crumbled (Whitlock, 2007, 279).

Additionally, the American submarines began scoring regular successes against large Japanese warships, up to and including aircraft carriers. The *USS Cavalla* under Herman Kossler sank the aircraft carrier *Shokaku* en route to the Battle of the Philippine Sea on June 18th, 1944, while the *USS Albacore* under James Blanchard torpedoed the carrier *Taiho* on the same day, putting it out of action.

More triumphs followed. The American submarines claimed three Japanese cruisers during the Battle of Leyte Gulf, and destroyed the battleship Kongo, on the pitch-black night of November 21st near Shanghai. The submarine *Sealion II* fired the deadly shots, and its skipper, Eli Reich, summed up the dramatic scene of the Kongo's demise tersely but effectively in his vessel's log: "Tremendous explosion dead ahead, it looked like a sunset at midnight. Radar reports battleship pip getting smaller – that it has disappeared. Battleship sunk – the sun set." (Wheeler, 1998, 183-184).

Sealion II

Early on the morning of November 29th, 1944, the *Balao*-class submarine *USS Archerfish* under Commander Joseph Enright achieved one of the most notable solo victories of the war. Lurking near the coast of Honshu near the small island of Inamba Shima, 90 miles south of Tokyo, the *Archerfish* suddenly made radar contact with a single aircraft carrier and a small band of escorts.

Moving to intercept, Enright saw a gigantic flattop looming out of the darkness, under an overcast sky lit from behind by the glow of a full moon. The *Archerfish* crept closer, while the Japanese ship moved almost directly towards the unseen peril on a zigzag course. Enright closed to engagement range and loosed a full salvo of six torpedoes from his vessel's forward tubes:

The sub's position was ideal –1,400-yards range almost on the target's starboard   beam so, at 0317, she commenced firing six "steam" torpedoes set for 10-foot depth.   Just 57 seconds after firing, the first fish hit close to the stern and a ball of flame   climbed the target's side. Ten seconds later Enright saw the second hit, then ducked   his scope and went deep to sweat out the expected beating. On the way down he   counted four more properly timed hits (Lockwood, 1951, 257).

The aircraft carrier, unbeknownst to Enright, represented a unique vessel, the *Shinano*. Built as a supercarrier on the hull of a third Yamato-class battleship as a last-minute conversion, the *Shinano* displaced 64,800 tons under standard load, making it the world's largest aircraft carrier ever as of 1944.

Each of the four torpedo hits smashed holes in the Shinano's hull, but the Japanese captain, believing the thick armor of the *Shinano* impervious to American Mark XIV torpedoes, ordered full speed ahead while the crew investigated the damage with little urgency. The high speed forced water into the breaches, creating swift internal flooding and forcing the openings in the hull to widen.

The Shinano soon foundered, rolling over after the captain gave the order to abandon ship. Major openings in the flight deck sucked in vast quantities of water and drew around 1,320 swimming Japanese sailors back inside to their doom. 1,080 men survived, though the Japanese government attempted to hide the *Shinano*'s loss from the public for two months.

Enright received credit for a 28,000 ton carrier with a similar outline to the *Shinano,* though he insisted the aircraft carrier he sank boasted much larger dimensions. No Americans knew of the *Shinano's* existence at that point in time, since the colossus represented a one-off modification of a rare super battleship class. Only after the war did the Navy learn of the giant's true identity and assign the correct credit to Enright, his crew, and the *Archerfish.*

During the final months of the war, Japan's fleet existed in such a reduced and tattered state that submarine actions grew rarer than they had been since early 1943. One of the last submarine actions involved the surrender of Japan's *I-401,* one of the country's huge I-400 submarines. The Japanese built the three subs in this class to serve as underwater aircraft carriers, featuring a watertight hangar housing three Aichi M6A1 Mountain Haze torpedo bombers.

The I-400 class submarines and the M6A1s constituted part of a scheme originally devised by Yamamoto to bomb New York City and Washington D.C. to demoralize the Americans. As the fortunes of war worsened, the IJN high command modified the plan, sending the submarines under Ariizumi – the unabashed war criminal who enjoyed butchering prisoners on his submarine deck and submerging to leave wounded survivors to drown or feed the sharks – to attack the Panama Canal, as the "God-Dragon Special Attack Squad."

The IJN aborted this mission in turn, directing the submarines to attack American ships anchored at Ulithi. Finally, the submarines attempted to return to Japan. Several days after the Emperor's surrender, I-401, under Ariizumi, the squadron commander, and Lieutenant Commander Nambu Nobukiyo, its skipper, found itself intercepted just short of Japan by the *Balao*-class submarine *USS Segundo.*

Ariizumi wanted to scuttle the I-401, but Nambu refused, preferring to save the lives of his 204 crew with the war already over. The submarine's officers decided to back Nambu, and the vessel surrendered, albeit with a face-saving arrangement whereby the submarine entered port under Japanese control. Ariizumi, however, could not endure the shame (and perhaps the thought of the war criminal's noose awaiting him following the repeated massacres he ordered during the war) and shot himself, leaving a suicide note: "As a professional, I have failed to fulfill my duties. This was my responsibility and I   am deeply sorry. With my death, I maintain the traditions of the Imperial Japanese   Navy and I take pride in having commanded a squadron that fought in the Pacific   until the end of the war. I am confident my crew will serve the country as loyal   subjects and I pray for the rebuilding of the Japanese Empire. Long live the   Emperor." (Geoghegan, 2013, 200).

Imperial Japan in World War II made use of the world's first dedicated suicide bombers, well ahead of the Islamic fanatics of the current day. The use of an explosive suicide to kill and demoralize the enemy took many forms. Japanese soldiers frequently pretended to surrender, while wearing rigged explosives under their clothes or carrying an armed grenade, attempting to get close enough to kill or wound a few Americans.

The famous kamikaze pilots, or "Divine Wind," likely constitute the most famous group of Imperial Japanese suicide bombers from the war. However, these men also possessed undersea counterparts – the pilots of Kaiten, or manned suicide torpedoes. First introduced in 1944, the Kaiten proved far less effective than the airborne kamikaze, though they inflicted high losses on the men selected to steer them.

Typically for the IJN, the Japanese researched close to a dozen variants of Kaiten. Only the Type 1 Kaiten saw actual production and use, however; the rest existed either as blueprints, or as test models which never reached the assembly line.

Initially built from a modified Type 93 "Long Lance" torpedo, a piece of ordnance massive enough to accommodate a crouching man in a cockpit amidships once the engineers made space by somewhat reducing the size of the warhead, Kaiten remained extremely touchy craft to operate.

The Japanese used air force pilots, rather than submarine sailors, to pilot the Kaiten, as their ergonomics and controls somewhat resembled those of a fighter plane. However, piloting always remained difficult. Even learning to use the devices proved lethal, with 15 men killed in accidents even under controlled conditions in a quiet bay: "Training in the Kaiten was hazardous. Each of the manned torpedoes had its own   idiosyncrasies which required constant attention. Tight controls, greased fittings,   and the close proximity of controls to one another was problematic. [...] The Kaiten were prone to dive or climb without warning. Sometimes they launched themselves   downward and stuck in the mud at the bottom of the bay." (Rielly, 2010, 94-95).

The problems of the Kaiten pilots only multiplied once launched under combat conditions. All Japanese suicide weapons, including kamikaze aircraft, Kaiten, suicide speedboats, and so forth represented an early effort to create "guided weapons," using a living human brain as the guidance computer. However, aircraft proved many times more effective in this role than the Kaiten, a nearly complete failure.

A Kaiten could descend as deep as 300 feet below the surface, but at that depth, water leaked steadily into the pilot's compartment. If the pilot failed to ascend, he might actually drown. Running at 180 feet below the surface provided a safe operational depth. However, during the approach run, the Kaiten pilot typically skimmed along just under the water at periscope depth so he could home in visually on his target, and descended to around 15 feet for the last hundred yards or so before impact.

Kaiten pilots usually closed on the target – up to 14 miles from the launching submarine, and sometimes more – at a lower cruising speed. When quite close, the pilot accelerated up to the suicide torpedo's top speed of approximately 35 mph in a last, desperate charge.

Due to the need to remain close to the surface to close with the target, Kaiten often suffered shelling from the American ships, which very frequently detonated the warhead and blew the craft to smithereens. In other cases, Kaiten struck reefs and exploded while trying reach anchored vessels, or suffered an involuntary crash dive due to mechanical problems and, in a shallow area, exploded when striking the bottom.

The Japanese claimed many kills for the Kaiten, based mainly on hearing the detonation of the device. However, most detonations resulted from U.S. Navy shellfire or depth charges, mechanical failures, or simply by running into objects other than their intended targets. The Kaiten pilots showed great eagerness, however, and consistently high morale – more so than the airborne kamikaze pilots, who eventually required considerable coercion to launch on their missions.

The first Kaiten attack ever proved the most successful. Submarine I-47 under Orita Zenji, a Kaiten carrier, approached the huge USN lagoon harbor at Ulithi Atoll on the night of November 19th-20th, 1944. The submarine commander gave his four Kaiten pilots a suitably ritualized sendoff: "[A] fine *sake*, a gift from the Emperor, was served in specially prepared lacquer-ware   cups. [...] At a speed of 12 knots I approached Ulithi. There was no need to take a star sight. The atoll sky was bright, like a coastal city's in peacetime. I told myself the presence of all those lights meant the enemy had no idea we were anywhere   near." (Wheeler, 1998, 116).

37 minutes after launch, the I-47's crew saw a tremendous flash and heard a thunderous report from inside the harbor. A second explosion followed 4 minutes later, at which point the submarine retired. Based purely on the sounds, the Japanese awarded the Kaiten pilots the destruction of an American battleship and an aircraft carrier!

In fact, the Kaiten destroyed a *Cimarron*-class oiler, the *USS Mississinewa*, AO-59, killing 63 men out of the ship's total complement of 299. A USN salvage team later recovered 2 million gallons of oil from the ship's tanks in 2003. The second explosion occurred when vigilant gunners on a nearby destroyer spotted the next Kaiten and scored a direct hit on it. The last two

Kaiten crashed into coral outcrops and their pilots drowned.

Though the Japanese launched 80 Kaiten over the remaining months of the war and claimed dozens of kills – counting each explosion heard over underwater microphones as a powerful American ship sent to the bottom – most of the pilots died uselessly. The only other "kill" consisted of the destroyer *USS Underhill,* on July 24th, 1945. The destroyer rammed a Kaiten after sinking its mothership, with the resulting explosion blowing the vessel in half instantly and killing 122 men, slightly less than half the crew.

A Kaiten struck Liberty Ship *Pontus H. Ross* while anchored near New Guinea on January 11th, 1945. The tiny submarine knocked a few hull plates askew, causing a minor leak in the hold, but did not explode and instead sank. A second Kaiten tried to attack the Ross, but suffered a catastrophic mechanical failure and exploded 100 yards away, though the shock of the blast bent the hull plates more and increased the leak slightly.

Beyond these three incidents, the Kaiten failed utterly to produce results other than the deaths of some Japanese pilots. Nevertheless, the Japanese built or modified 25 submarines to act as Kaiten carriers, capable of carrying 2, 4, 5, or 6 Kaiten depending on their exact configuration. These vessels represented part of the Empire's last-ditch effort to change the course of the Pacific War and, like many of the other increasingly bizarre weapons developed, signally failed to halt or even slow the U.S. Navy's relentless advance.

In the end, one submarine fleet contributed significantly to victory, while the other, despite inflicting random and sometimes extensive damage, did almost nothing to alter the overall course of the war or even slow its adversary's onrush. Doctrine, employment, and even culture played a role in this immense difference. Though also thirsting to destroy capital ships, the Americans unleashed their submarines to wreak havoc on all types of Japanese shipping, operating independently and making the most of the weapons system's possibilities.

All the while, the Japanese accepted authority with fatalistic, uncomplaining obedience. No submarine skipper ever banged on Yamamoto Isoroku's desk and told him that he was being a fool to use his submarines in the manner prescribed. Receiving no feedback from the lower ranks due to their profoundly authoritarian culture, the Japanese high naval command existed in a hermetic echo chamber wherein the fact that their strategy utterly wasted a superb and powerful submarine force could never be brought to their attention.

As a result, the *Gato*-class and *Balao*-class submarines tore into the soft underbelly of Japanese shipping like a frenzied swarm of piranhas, while the I-boats lumbered about futilely like whale sharks, huge and impressive but nearly useless in the overall war effort.

Online Resources

Other World War II titles by Charles River Editors

Other titles about World War II submarines on Amazon

Bibliography

Blair, Clay. *Hitler's U-Boat War: The Hunters, 1939-1942*. New York, 1996.

Blair, Clay. *Hitler's U-Boat War: The Hunted, 1942-1945*. New York, 1998.

Budiansky, Stephen. *Blackett's War: The Men who Defeated the Nazi U-Boats and Brought Science to the Art of Warfare*. New York, 2013.

Collingwood, Donald. *The Captain Class Frigates in the Second World War*. Annapolis, 1999.

Doenitz, Karl, and R.H. Stevens (translator). *Memoirs: Ten Years and Twenty Days*. Annapolis, 1990.

Howard, Peter. *Underwater Raid on Tirpitz*. Hersham, 2006.

Hoyt, Edwin P. *The U-Boat Wars*. New York, 1984.

Huges, Francis Massie. *Action Report on the Operations Concerning the Loss by Enemy Action of the U.S.S. BLOCK ISLAND on 29 May 1944*. Cruise report; http://www.uboatarchive.net/U-549A/U-549BlockIslandReport.htm; retrieved March 23rd, 2016; original report June 29th, 1944.

McCartney, Innes. *British Submarines 1939-45*. Oxford, 2008.

McKee, Fraser M. "An Explosive Story: The Rise and Fall of the Common Depth Charge." *The Northern Mariner*, III, No. 1, January 1993, pp. 45-58.

O'Brien, Phillips Payson. *How the War was Won: Air-Sea Power and Allied Victory in World War II*. Cambridge, 2015.

Paterson, Lawrence. *Weapons of Desperation: German Frogmen and Midget Submarines of the Second World War*. London, 2006.

Peillard, Leonce and Oliver Coburn (translator). *Sink the Tirpitz!* London, 1983.

Prenatt, Jamie and Mark Stille. *Axis Midget Submarines, 1939-1945*. Oxford, 2014.

Squadron/Signal Publications. *Escort Carriers in Action*. Carrollton, 1996.

Steinmetz, Everett H. "USS Barb (55-220) and Subron 50." *POLARIS magazine,* June 1998 Issue.

Turner, David. *Last Dawn: The Royal Oak Tragedy at Scapa Flow.* Ely, 2008.

Warren, C.E.T. and James Benson. *The Midget Raiders: the Wartime Story of Human Torpedoes and Midget Submarines.* New York, 1954.

Werner, Herbert A. *Iron Coffins: A Personal Account of the German U-Boat Battles of World War II.* New York, 2002.

Williamson, Gordon. *Wolf Pack: the Story of the U-Boat in World War II.* Oxford, 2005.

CPSIA information can be obtained
at www.ICGtesting.com
Printed in the USA
LVHW02s2347200118
563363LV00033B/759/P